Simply H

Simply Hegel

ROBERT L. WICKS

SIMPLY CHARLY
NEW YORK

Contents

Praise for *Simply Hegel*

"Robert Wicks has achieved the near-miracle of presenting the whole of Hegel's thought in a way that will both enlighten the novice and be of great interest to seasoned Hegel buffs for its originality and insight. Wicks's esteem for Hegel is evident throughout; he writes from the heart as well as the intellect."
  –Michael Inwood, author of A *Hegel Dictionary* and Emeritus Fellow, Trinity College, University of Oxford

"Hegel is a notoriously difficult philosopher to approach on one's own. This brief introduction offers a useful companion to those making the effort: after opening a window on Hegel's life and times, Wicks gives a helpful reading of some of the most crucial moments within Hegel's writings, including key sections of the *Phenomenology of Spirit* and *Encyclopedia*. And, in nicely emphasizing the dynamic, practical and ultimately comprehensive character of Hegelian thought, Wicks suggests–perhaps most importantly of all–some of the reasons why his work still matters so much to us philosophically."
  –C. Allen Speight, Associate Professor of Philosophy, Boston University

"Hegel is one of the world's most important–and most difficult–philosophers. This short book brings these ideas to life in real simplicity that would help spark future interest in his groundbreaking ideas."
  –Thom Brooks, Professor of Law and Government at Durham University and Dean of Durham Law School

"This short book, which outlines G.W.F. Hegel's main ideas,

summarizes the philosophical works and positions with clear non-technical language while maintaining the dominant threads and principles of explanation that carry throughout Hegel's systematic philosophy. Indeed, Robert Wicks's highlighting of Hegel's view that all of reality is a complex process of growth and development is mirrored in the author's own tracing of the development of Hegel's philosophical positions, from the earliest to the last of his writings. By accentuating the biographical, historical, and intellectual context of Hegel's thought, *Simply Hegel* provides an excellent introduction–simply but not oversimplified–that will be accessible to anyone new to Hegel, as well as a helpful refresher for those who already have some familiarity with this great thinker."

–**David A. Duquette, author of Hegel's History of Philosophy: New Interpretations and Professor Emeritus, St. Norbert College**

"*Simply Hegel* is an extraordinary achievement. Robert Wicks manages to explicate Hegel's multifaceted system and convoluted arguments in ways that are grounded in scholarship, enlightening, sympathetic and humorous. This book is welcome to anyone trying to make plausible Hegel's thinking to first (and second, and third) time readers of it. Whether one approaches Hegel from the traditional perspective of the *Phenomenology of Spirit* or from that of the *Encyclopaedia* system, Wicks's contribution helps seeing the wood beyond the trees while whetting readers' appetite for studying the trees as well."

–**Allegra de Laurentiis, Professor of Philosophy, State University of New York at Stony Brook**

Other *Great Lives*

Series Editor's Foreword

S imply Charly's "Great Lives" series offers brief but authoritative introductions to the world's most influential people–scientists, artists, writers, economists, and other historical figures whose contributions have had a meaningful and enduring impact on our society.

Each book provides an illuminating look at the works, ideas, personal lives, and the legacies these individuals left behind, also shedding light on the thought processes, specific events, and experiences that led these remarkable people to their groundbreaking discoveries or other achievements. Additionally, every volume explores various challenges they had to face and overcome to make history in their respective fields, as well as the little-known character traits, quirks, strengths, and frailties, myths and controversies that sometimes surrounded these personalities.

Our authors are prominent scholars and other top experts who have dedicated their careers to exploring each facet of their subjects' work and personal lives.

Unlike many other works that are merely descriptions of the major milestones in a person's life, the "Great Lives" series goes above and beyond the standard format and content. It brings substance, depth, and clarity to the sometimes-complex lives and works of history's most powerful and influential people.

We hope that by exploring this series, readers will not only gain new knowledge and understanding of what drove these geniuses, but also find inspiration for their own lives. Isn't this what a great book is supposed to do?

Charles Carlini, Simply Charly
New York City

Preface

G eorg Wilhelm Friedrich Hegel was one of the world's greatest philosophers, and anyone who approaches his writings for the first time will inevitably be puzzled. Indeed, people who have studied his work for decades still labor to decipher the meaning of certain passages. At the same time, there is an amazing simplicity that underlies Hegel's thought: he saw the universe as a single being that is growing into maturity; humans are the leading lights in this growth, as we work together to build a more rational, morally balanced society. His vision is a tremendous and inspiring one for anyone who looks forward to world peace.

Since the time of Hegel's death in 1831, there have been many readers and interpreters of his 20 volumes of writings. Renditions of his philosophy are assorted, and corresponding differences of opinion as to what his most important insights were–differences of opinion about "what is living and what is dead"–are notable in contemporary Hegel scholarship.

This book is entitled "simply" Hegel. It presents a traditional reading of Hegel as a supreme metaphysician who formulated one of the most impressive and comprehensive philosophical systems in the history of human thought. These days, it is no longer popular to compose grand philosophical systems, but it was standard practice to do so during the early 19th-century when he lived. This book tries to respect the spirit in which this great philosopher formulated his thoughts, and does not follow contemporary fashion, which sometimes departs radically from the tradition in which Hegel wrote. The hope is to present in outline Hegel's views as they were originally intended to be understood, acknowledging that this is an unattainable ideal that can only be approximated, if only because we live with the perspective of a different century.

This book presents "simply" Hegel in another sense as well. Rather than working through the complex details of his arguments in sequence, as would an advanced and lengthy study, *Simply Hegel* sums up his main ideas, sometimes with diagrams and charts, along with accompanying examples to illustrate his insights. The aim is to present Hegel's philosophy in a straightforward, easily understandable, and yet substantially useful and meaningful way, establishing a foundation for further study, if that is desired. As the book works through the contents of his philosophical development and writings, it emphasizes how Hegel's message can apply constructively to one's life and fundamental attitudes, and perhaps even change them. The conclusion offers a set of prescriptions from Hegel's philosophy that can apply constructively to our own lives.

I owe a profound debt to the people with whom I studied and conversed about Hegel over the years. These include my teacher at the University of Wisconsin-Madison, and now good friend, Ivan Soll; my instructors, Christoph Jamme and Helmut Schneider, many years ago when I was a student at the Hegel-Archives in Bochum, Germany; my classmate from graduate school and fine Hegel scholar, Ken Westphal, who I've known for decades; and Bob Solomon, an outstanding human being and philosopher in so many respects, who visited Auckland frequently when he was alive and taught so inspiringly as a visitor in my classes. My greatest debt is to my many students who attended my undergraduate class on Kant and Hegel at the University of Auckland, and to the University of Auckland itself. Without them, I would never have been inspired to understand and communicate Hegel's views as best as I could.

My first class in Hegel—it was a philosophy of history class—was at Michigan State University, taught by Richard Peterson, where we read Hegel's lectures on the history of philosophy. It was the most eye-opening book for me, since it described the course of world history from beginning to end as a single narrative. Never had I seen how human history could make sense. I was not in the position to be critical at the time, but this book had a constructive effect on my appreciation for philosophical systems of thought. Prior to that experience, I had been immersed in the study of Ludwig Wittgenstein's philosophy of language under the guidance of Ronald

Suter, one of my first and most authentic professors of philosophy and true Wittgensteinian in the best sense of the word.

Upon attending graduate school at the University of Wisconsin-Madison, I was exposed to some highly accomplished and influential scholars who specialized in causal and information-based theories of knowledge, mind, and meaning. That path changed in a couple of years after I took a graduate course on Hegel's *Phenomenology* with Ivan Soll, who reawakened my interest in this philosopher. Working thereafter with Ivan, Bill Hay, and Don Crawford, whose expertise in Kant's aesthetics gave me a solid background for understanding Hegel from a Kantian perspective, I decided to write a Ph.D. thesis on Hegel's aesthetics under Don's supervision. The comparison and contrast between Kant's and Hegel's philosophies formed the basis for all my subsequent studies.

On a more recent note, I would like to thank Charles Carlini, whose editorial support and understanding during the composition of this book has been so impeccably first-rate. It has been a pleasure to work with Charles and to have been given the opportunity to communicate Hegel's views to others through this book.

Robert L. Wicks
Auckland, New Zealand

Acknowledgements

A ll the images contained herein are from copyright-free resources. I would nonetheless like to thank those who produced or reproduced the images that appear in this book, namely, Putzgers Historischer Schul-Atlas, 1905 (Map of the Holy Roman Empire), Der Zinnmann [The Tinman] (Hegel's Birthplace in Stuttgart), Christoph Braun (portrait of Hegel, from a painting by Ernst Hader [1866-1922] on a photograph card by Sophus Williams [1835-1900]), Christian Thiele (painting of Hölderlin by Franz Karl Hiemer [1768-1822]), Claxon (painting of Schelling by Christian Friedrich Tieck [1776-1851]), Metilsteiner (Scene After the Battle of Jena, "Teile der zerstörten Wohnhäuser in der Jüdengasse in Jena, nach dem Brand durch Artilleriebeschuss," c. 1810, image from the Thüringer Monatsblätter, June 1916, p. 35), LeastCommonAncestor (Melanchton-Gymnasium, copperplate by Johann Adam Delsenbach [1687-1765]), A. Carse (The University of Berlin), Was a bee (Brain in the Vat), unknown (Immanuel Kant), sman_5 (the Acropolis in Athens), Wikimedia Commons (Descartes), Steinninn (Christ Giving his Blessing by Hans Memling [1430-1494]), AnnieCee (The Lord is My Good Shepherd, painting by Bernhard Plockhorst [1825-1907]), Gmcfoley (Christ Carrying the Cross, painting by El Greco [1541-1614]), JoJan (The Battle of Jena, colored lithograph by Charles Horace Vernet [1758-1836] and Jacques François Swebach [1769-1823]), Internet Archive Book Images (Metamorphosis of the Monarch butterfly, 1907, in Evolution in Animal Life, by David Starr Jordan and Vernon L. Kellogg, D. Appleton and Co.), Kiko2000 (Hegel's Grave at Dorotheenstädtischer Friedhof, Berlin, Germany), Marie-Lan Nguyen (silver tetradrachm), Wikimedia Commons (Head of Apollo), Andreas Praefcke (Handshake with the Eye of God, wood sculpture). The photograph of Hegel's desk is my own. Some of the images I have cropped, sharpened, brightened, and/or otherwise adjusted in a standard, non-distortive way to improve their appearance.

1. Hegel's Life and Times

Hegel was born in the city of Stuttgart on August 27, 1770—the same year as the composer Ludwig van Beethoven (1770-1827), the English poet William Wordsworth (1770-1850), and the German poet, Friedrich Hölderlin (1770-1843), with whom Hegel would become good friends. Hegel is known correctly as a German philosopher, but the country that we now know as Germany did not exist during his lifetime. The German territory was then part of the Holy Roman Empire, which was a complex collection of kingdoms, duchies, and other domains ruled by monarchs under the authority of the Holy Roman Emperor. The Empire originated with the reign of Charlemagne (800-824) and dissolved in 1806 in the aftermath of a decisive battle in December 1805 between Napoleon's army and the Russians and Austrians at Austerlitz, in the present-day Czech Republic. When Hegel was born, the Holy Roman Emperor was Joseph II, the "king of Germany" and of other lands, who ruled from 1765 to 1790.

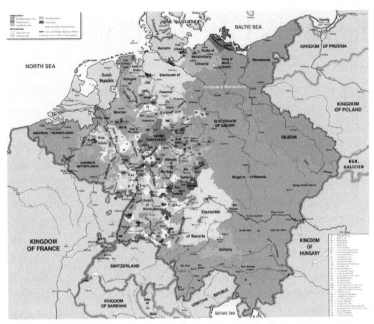

The Holy Roman Empire in 1789 at the time of the French Revolution, when Hegel was 19 years old

Hegel's birthplace, Stuttgart, was in the Duchy of Württemberg near the Black Forest area of today's southwestern Germany. His family was of sound social status, neither extremely wealthy nor impoverished, but well-educated, comfortable, and respectable. His father worked in the financial offices of the Duke of Württemberg and his mother was the daughter of a successful lawyer. Hegel was very close to his mother, who taught him Latin when he was young. She died when he was 13. Hegel—his parents called him Wilhelm—attended a good elementary school, was always the first in his class, and was expected to lead a professional life, most likely within the church or possibly in law. He had a younger sister and brother, Christiane Luise (1773-1832) and Georg Ludwig (1776-1812). His brother later lost his life as an officer fighting for Napoleon during the French attack on Russia. Christiane committed suicide not long after learning about Hegel's death.

One of the literary works that significantly influenced Hegel when he was a teenager was the play, *Nathan the Wise* (1779), written by Gotthold Ephraim Lessing (1729-1781). The play takes place in medieval Jerusalem during the time of the crusades, and interrelates characters from three religions—Judaism, Christianity, and Islam. Its message is that historical differences between religions do not matter; what is important in God's eyes is a person's morality. In this respect, religions are said to be in fundamental agreement with one another insofar as they urge people to lead good, moral lives. Human reason allows us to see that in their moral substance, the religions are spiritually the same.

Hegel's Birthplace in Stuttgart, now a Hegel Museum

After graduating from high school, Hegel enrolled in the theological seminary attached to the University of Tübingen, about 25 miles south from his home. This was the Tübinger Stift, associated with the Evangelical-Lutheran church, to which Hegel affirmed in his application the intention to become a theologian. He declared that in future he hoped to serve the Duke of Württemberg wherever he might need him, whether in churches, schools, or in the foreign service.

The Tübinger Stift

Hegel attended the Tübinger Stift for five years, from the age of 18 to 23 (1788-1793), where he studied mathematics, history, psychology, physics, classical languages, logic, philosophy, and theology. He roomed with Friedrich Hölderlin and Friedrich Wilhelm Joseph Schelling (1775-1854), both of whom would later become renowned—Hölderlin as a poet, and Schelling as a philosopher. After they graduated, Hegel would spend significant time with both of them.

Three Roommates: Hegel, Hölderlin, Schelling

Not long after their studies began, France was shaken by a revolution whose effects reverberated throughout Europe. It started in 1789, when the French king, Louis XVI recalled into session a political entity dormant since 1614—the Estates General—to help resolve the country's serious financial problems. The Estates General was constituted of representatives of the three "estates"—the First Estate (clergy), the Second Estate (nobles), and the Third Estate (95 percent of the population).

Due to immediate disagreements about how the voting would take place, since the outcome on this matter would imply which Estate would prevail in the decision making, the Third Estate formed its own governmental group, the National Assembly. Its activities soon led to the overthrow of the nobility and the establishment of a republic, governed by democratic ideals. As the years went by, the revolution became violent, with shocking executions in 1793 of the king and queen, Marie Antoinette. The following year, a massive number of beheadings took place during the "Reign of Terror," for which the guillotine became famous.

At the revolution's outset, one of the key documents of the Assembly was the "Declaration of the Rights of Man and of the Citizen," from August 1789. It was written by the Marquis de Lafayette in collaboration with Thomas Jefferson, the author of the American Declaration of Independence, who was in Paris at the time. The following Article is exemplary:

> **Article VI** – The law is the expression of the general will. All the citizens have the right of contributing personally or through their representatives to its formation. It must be the same for all, either that it protects, or that it punishes. All the citizens, being equal in its eyes, are equally admissible to all public dignities, places, and employments, according to their capacity and without distinction other than that of their virtues and of their talents.

It is noteworthy that these ideas continued to inspire people into the next two centuries. One notable example is Martin Luther King when he spoke to a crowd of over 200,000 people in Washington D. C. in August 1963, saying, "I have a dream that my four little children will one day live in a nation where they will not be judged by the color of their skin but by the content of their character." With similar force, Hegel and many of his contemporaries were inspired by the French Revolutionary ideals of liberty, equality, and fraternity. Influential to the French Revolution and to Hegel as well, was *The Social Contract* (1762) by Jean-Jacques Rousseau (1712-1778), a work that 20 years earlier had set the intellectual stage for the revolution, and which Hegel was often seen reading for inspiration in Tübingen.

Hegel's thoughts on religion, Kant's influence

After Hegel graduated from the Tübinger Stift, he obtained a position as a live-in tutor for the children of an aristocratic family in Bern, Switzerland, about 150 miles in a straight line, (but longer by road) from Stuttgart. He began in October 1793 at age 23, leaving Bern at the end of 1796.

Shortly before traveling to Bern, Hegel wrote an essay on religion—it is known as the "Tübingen Fragment"—where he emphasized the importance of having a personal, spiritual feeling for God and religious matters, as opposed to being mainly concerned with rituals and externally-oriented religious practices. This is expressed by the difference, for instance, between saying a heartfelt prayer of gratitude when walking peacefully through the forest by oneself, and dressing up impeccably for a Sunday service, simply to look socially proper and upstanding.

Hegel believed that the truth of religion resides in one's heart, rather than in external appearances, but he also appreciated that religions prescribe abstract moral rules to guide people's lives. Although these rules are important in their generality, prescriptions such as "do not steal," "do not dishonor one's parents," or more philosophically, "do not act irrationally," still need to be connected concretely to daily life. Trying to bridge this contrast between "outer rules" and "inner feeling" was a task that continued throughout Hegel's intellectual life, as he explored various ways to connect abstract truths with lived experience.

While in Bern, Hegel continued to write about the difficulties facing Christianity, for he was seeing that many people lacked a heartfelt feeling for religion, concerned superficially, as they were, with rituals and other external practices, thinking that was what religion is mainly all about. Not all Christians were like this—perhaps the Quakers were an exception—but Hegel was noticing that Christianity was losing its inspirational force in his part of the world. It was a common perception, which inspired many writers to explore Christianity's roots by studying the historical Jesus, hoping to rediscover the living essence of Christianity by understanding who Jesus was as a person. Among Hegel's writings in Bern were two book-length manuscripts entitled *The Life of Jesus* (1795) and *The Positivity of the Christian Religion* (1796), where he tried to comprehend who Jesus was. Influential for both works was Immanuel Kant's moral theory, which Hegel was then reading and advocating.

Respecting the classical idea that humans are essentially rational beings and that rationality is the best part of us, Kant formulated a moral theory based on reason alone, valid independently of physical facts such as the temperature at which water boils, the number of chemical elements, the distance from the earth to the sun, etc., as well as details of historical matters. Kant's aim was to present a moral theory that applies to everyone at all times and places, no matter where, when, or how a person lives. He maintained that being moral is a matter of living in accord with our inherent rationality, which he understood as acting in a consistent manner, rather than a contradictory one.

According to Kant, an absolute moral command or "categorical imperative" resides within us as rational beings; in this context, "categorical" means "absolute," and "imperative" means "command." This categorical imperative is to always act in such manner that the principle (or "maxim") of one's action could be made into a universal law. It says, in effect, that moral standards apply equally to everyone, urging all people to "be reasonable." It is not morally permissible for governmental officials, or the extremely wealthy, or the extremely influential, to act criminally and remain free from prosecution, while ordinary citizens are brought to trial and imprisoned for the same actions, because moral standards are the same for everyone.

For Kant, to act morally is to act from a feeling of respect for oneself as a rational being. Since we are not perfectly rational beings and have animalistic inclinations as well, our moral feeling assumes the form of a respect for duty, as we appreciate what is best in us and realize that we sometimes cannot live up to how we ought to be.

In his *Life of Jesus*, Hegel presents Jesus as someone who appreciates that in our rationality, human beings have within themselves the means to determine right and wrong, and have no need to appeal to external authorities for moral guidance. He describes Jesus as asking the people to whom he spoke, not to follow his words because they come from him as a religious authority, but to follow his words after having subjected them carefully to their own judgment and reason. He has Jesus stating

Kant's categorical imperative almost word-for-word. As Kant was born in the 18th century, Jesus's sermons could not have contained Kantian phrases but Hegel perceived that Kant's moral theory conveys the essence of Jesus's message, as one might formulate that message philosophically.

After Hegel left Bern, he moved to Frankfurt where Hölderlin was living, securing work as a tutor in the household of a wine merchant. He spent much time with Hölderlin, exchanging philosophical ideas and developing their friendship. More inclined towards a poetic view of life, Hölderlin stimulated Hegel to refresh some of the views he had expressed in his "Tübingen Fragment" that emphasized the importance of feeling. This was not merely a rarefied sense of duty or self-respect as we have in Kant's moral theory, but that of rich emotions. Through his discussions with Hölderlin, Hegel realized that his interest in Kant's moral theory had led him to downplay the importance of human feeling; in Kant's philosophy, feelings are mostly set aside as too fleshly, variable, and unsuitable for expressing what is universal, necessary, and identical in everyone.

While in Frankfurt, Hegel accordingly adopted a more "romantic," as opposed to "Kantian," attitude. At this time—he was in Frankfurt from 1797 to 1800, ages 27-30—he wrote a third book entitled *The Spirit of Christianity and its Fate* (1799), in which he reconsidered the nature of Christianity, emphasizing this time the importance of love as opposed to abstract and universal moral principles as we find in Kant. We will say more about Hegel's transition from Kantianism to romanticism in Chapter 3.

With Hegel's father's death in 1799, along with Hölderlin's involvement in a love affair that absorbed his attention, Hegel left Frankfurt. After writing to Schelling, his other roommate at Tübingen, who had done well for himself in Jena as a university professor, Hegel was given the opportunity to work with him, arriving in Jena in 1801. Although Hegel had already completed three book manuscripts, he had chosen not to publish them, so outward appearances were suggesting that among the three roommates, Hegel, who was 30 at the time, was falling behind and needed some help. Hölderlin had been publishing his poetry, and Schelling had already secured a professorship.

Hegel came into his own in Jena, completing, by 1806, what would be one of his most famous and influential books, the *Phenomenology of Spirit*. Leading up to this, Hegel worked closely with Schelling, writing philosophical articles and a monograph in support of Schelling's views, as well as collaborating with him as co-editor of a philosophical journal. In 1803, Schelling left Jena for Würzburg—a city about 100 miles away—to work at another university, leaving Hegel behind. This gave Hegel—a thinker whose intellectual powers matched Schelling's—the room to develop his own views. Hegel's position at the university nonetheless remained difficult: for most of his time there, he was a private teacher—a *Privatdozent*—whose income came from the small donations of the students in his classes.

Jena had been a center of German romanticism in the years prior to Hegel's arrival, and Schelling was personally close to the city's romantic thinkers. Hegel's own attitude towards romanticism, however, was mixed: from his days in Tübingen and his friendship with Hölderlin, he recognized the importance of feelings such as love; at the same time, he remained an enthusiast of the rationality-grounded ideals of the French revolution and of philosophies based on reason, rather than feeling or direct intuition. Now finding himself free to reflect on this tension in the absence of any commitments to Schelling, Hegel worked on constructing a philosophy that could take both concrete feelings and abstract principles into account.

By 1806, political tensions had become pronounced with Napoleon's power having increased to the point of threatening the disintegration of the Holy Roman Empire—an "agglomeration" which Voltaire described in 1756 as neither "holy," nor "Roman" nor an "empire." Prussia, working against Napoleon in a coalition with Great Britain, Russia, Saxony, and Sweden, was soon waging war with France, and a decisive battle took place in October in the area surrounding Jena. After Napoleon defeated the Prussians, Hegel had little choice but to leave the city, for despite his enthusiasm for the French, he had little money and dim prospects for continued employment at the university. The University of Jena was one of the few that remained open after Napoleon's victory, but it became a barebones operation.

After the Battle of Jena: A Drawing of a Burned-Out Street in the City Center, near the Eichplatz, October 1806

Professional success

Through the help of a friend, Hegel found a job as a newspaper editor in Bamberg—a city about 100 miles away, where *Phenomenology's* publishers were located. Working for the *Bamberger Zeitung* enabled Hegel to support himself after having hit financial rock bottom in Jena. It was not his ideal position, but neither was it problematic: the newspaper provided an income and an opportunity for Hegel to express his pro-French sentiments through the articles it printed.

After a year and a half at the newspaper, Hegel was appointed to be headmaster of the Melanchthon-Gymnasium (high school) in Nuremberg—an institution still in existence whose history reaches back to 1526—where he also taught some philosophy. With this return to the world of academic institutions, the position was more to his liking, and he remained in Nuremberg for seven years, until 1816. He married Marie von Tucher, settled down, and had two sons, Karl and Thomas Immanuel (a daughter died soon after birth).

The Phenomenology of Spirit, which Hegel completed just before leaving Jena, set the scene for his mature philosophy, as he intended to integrate abstract thought (logic), the physical world (nature), and human culture (spirit) into a complete philosophical system. The first segment, the Science of Logic, written while Hegel was in Nuremberg, was an extensive and dense book of over one thousand pages. He published it in three segments: the first segment (334 pages) appeared in 1812, the second (282 pages) in 1813, and the third (403 pages) in 1816. It was, and still is, a supreme work, and in time, it confirmed Hegel's reputation as an outstanding philosopher. One can appreciate Hegel's impressive intellectual powers and capabilities: while he was writing the Science of Logic, he was engaged in his daily job as headmaster in conjunction with a second position as a school inspector; he was also teaching his courses and managing a family.

The Melanchthon-Gymnasium in Nuremberg (the large building at the right-center)

The years during which Hegel was in Nuremberg were politically charged within the wider European scene. In his attack on Russia in 1812, Napoleon suffered a defeat that cost him most of his army. He abdicated his position as emperor in April 1814 and although he made a dramatic comeback to power almost a year later in March 1815, it did not last long: the British and Prussians defeated him in Belgium at the Battle of Waterloo in June 1815.

In Hegel's vicinity, Napoleon's defeat precipitated shifts in the attitudes of the governing bodies that made Nuremberg a less attractive place for him to live. Another factor motivating a change was his personal and enduring interest in securing a position as a university professor, for he was not content to remain a high school rector for the rest of his life. In 1816, at age 46, Hegel's wishes came to fruition when he obtained a position as a professor of philosophy at the University of Heidelberg, almost a decade after his departure from Jena.

Hegel's life in Heidelberg was comfortable, and it included scenic trips with his wife amid the regular university social events. He also had pleasurable visits by the German romantic writer Jean Paul (1763-1825) and the French philosopher, Victor Cousin (1792-1867), who was then a young man. Hegel was also the editor of a philosophical journal and, most importantly, he completed his system of philosophy, which was published in 1817 as the *Encyclopedia of the Philosophical Sciences.* The three-volume work was composed of (1) Logic, (2) The Philosophy of Nature, and (3) The Philosophy of Spirit.

The first volume of the *Encyclopedia,* "Logic," is an abridged version of *The Science of Logic*—it is sometimes called the "smaller logic"—that, like its predecessor, systematically organizes the sphere of purely abstract concepts as they appear in metaphysical speculation and traditional logic. This sphere includes concepts such as "being," "nothing," "becoming," "essence," and "substance." The second volume, The Philosophy of Nature, discusses physical, chemical, and biological concepts in sequence as a prelude to the emergence of human beings. Completing the system, the third volume, The Philosophy of Spirit, addresses in sequence matters concerning human society, such as psychology, property, rights, morality, the family and the state. The Philosophy of Spirit culminates in a section on "absolute spirit," which is constituted by art, religion, and philosophy. As is evident from this list of contents, Hegel's *Encyclopedia* tried to cover the entire field of academic knowledge as it was recognized during his time.

With his reputation solidified through his books and university service, it was not long before Hegel received an invitation from the University of Berlin to assume the most prestigious professorship in the German realm: to fill the vacant chair of Johann Gottlieb Fichte (1762-1814), who had been a major presence in German philosophy and who had died a few years earlier. This appointment crowned Hegel's career, and it initiated a period of fruitful academic productivity and fame that would carry him through to his death in 1831.

Final years

In 1820, Hegel published his fourth and final book, *Elements of the Philosophy of Right*, which elaborated on the section of *The Philosophy of Spirit* that concerned social and political topics. It discussed property, contracts, morality, marriage, family, community, police, state, international law, and world history. Since the days of the French Revolution and throughout his career, Hegel had been interested in political events, and he often engaged in debates about laws, constitutions, judicial decisions, and governmental policies. This book represented his mature ideas on subjects related to civic matters.

Hegel's collected works amount to over 20 volumes, and one might ask what these volumes contain, if he published only four books during his career (or five, if one includes the monograph on Fichte and Schelling that he wrote in Jena). A large portion are transcripts of the classroom lectures he gave at the University of Berlin on world history, fine art, religion, and the history of philosophy. They are extensive: his lectures on fine art alone are approximately 1200 pages in length.

The main topics of these Berlin lectures—art, religion, and philosophy, all considered in their historical development—are at the highest point in Hegel's philosophy as components of "absolute spirit." They are "absolute" in the sense that if one wants to understand the leading, most important, and spiritually governing ideas of any given society, then one should look at the society's art, religion, and philosophy, for this is where those ideas are given the most direct expression. As such, history, art, religion, and philosophy were of primary concern to Hegel, and he devoted considerable energy to them in his university lectures.

The University of Berlin

The University of Berlin

While in Berlin, Hegel had the opportunity to travel to other parts of Europe, where he experienced diverse cultures first-hand. He especially enjoyed visiting the art museums in the larger cities, which included Dresden, Amsterdam, Vienna, Paris, and Prague. In Paris, where he saw his friend Victor Cousin once more, his experience was particularly memorable: in addition to his visit to the Louvre museum, Paris recalled his early identification with the French revolution and its leading ideas.

In 1830, Hegel was elected to the position of rector of the University of Berlin, the highest administrative position in the institution, equivalent to the university president. He had been dean of the philosophy faculty some years earlier in 1821. As evident from his success in university service, his years as rector of the Melanchthon-Gymnasium in Nuremberg had served Hegel well in developing his administrative talents. His philosophical views had its adherents and its critics, and his life at the university had sometimes been turbulent due to his friendships with politically-controversial figures such as Victor Cousin, but in the end, Hegel rose to the top of his profession and became the head of his academic institution.

It is unfortunate that Hegel did not have much longer to live, for in 1831 a stomach ailment that had been troubling him for some time intensified and led to his death on November 14 of that year. The timing of his passing coincided with a cholera epidemic that was spreading to Berlin from Russia, and he was first thought to have died from that illness.

Hegel was survived by his wife Marie, two sons that he had with her, Karl and Thomas Immanuel, and another son, Ludwig, who he had out of wedlock with Christiana Burkhardt while in Jena. Ludwig died coincidentally in 1831 as well, while serving in the Dutch army in Indonesia. Neither Hegel nor Ludwig knew of each other's deaths when they passed away. Hegel's sister, Christiane, whose mental health over the years showed evidence of being fragile, committed suicide on February 2, 1832, less than three months after her brother's death.

In a quarter of a decade, Hegel rose from a virtually penniless, relatively unknown, unemployed professor at the University of Jena, to become the rector of the University of Berlin and one of the most renowned philosophers of his time.

2. Self-Consciousness

As human beings, what makes us importantly different from dogs, cats, frogs, fish, and all the other animals? One difference is that a dog, for instance, has no idea that it lives within a solar system located within the Milky Way galaxy, on a planet we call "Earth." Dogs cannot contemplate the stars as we do. They live mainly in the moment, not realizing that their days are precisely numbered. They have no idea that they will eventually pass away. They can neither read nor write and they are unable to tell jokes. To a dog, there is no perplexity about why it is here in the world. Its existence is an innocent one.

The Bible expresses this difference between humans and other living things in the Book of Genesis. Describing our special place in the world, it is said that God gave humans the responsibility to take care of all other living beings whose awareness is less advanced. In ancient Greece, we find a similar view. The Greeks appreciated how humans are self-conscious beings and especially how they are rational beings, and how these features give us a higher status and more responsible place in the world.

For centuries thereafter in the history of Western philosophy, self-consciousness and rationality have been regarded as our most valuable and unique features. When humans are referred to as having been made in God's image, our self-consciousness and rationality are usually in mind, as well as our freedom, thought to derive from our ability to reflect.

Indeed, self-consciousness, rationality, and freedom have been regarded as divine. Many people conceive of God as a self-conscious and intelligent being, and as a supreme and benevolent monarch and artist, who chose freely to create the world in which we live. The best part of the human being is accordingly considered to reflect God. Hegel respected this way of understanding our place in the world, although he developed it in his own way to a point where, as we will see, it becomes unclear whether one would refer to his philosophy as "theistic," or as involving God in any traditional manner.

At the beginning of the scientific age, in the philosophy of the 1600s and 1700s, self-consciousness was a fundamental starting-point for thinking critically about what we know. A leading representative of this approach is René Descartes (1596-1650), who became well known through his *Meditations on First Philosophy* (1641). Descartes lived during a period in Europe when people were beginning to experience a sharp tension between statements in the Bible and the new results of scientific inquiry. There was a question of whether one should respect Biblical teachings, or the conflicting propositions that were emerging from the use of scientific instruments such as telescopes, microscopes, barometers, and thermometers.

Descartes's method of doubt

As a sign of the times, Descartes's contemporary, the great astronomer Galileo Galilei (1564-1642), was put on trial for asserting what we now accept as fact, namely, that the sun is at the center of the solar system and that the planets revolve around the sun. Descartes held the same belief, but after he learned about Galileo's arrest, he hesitated to publish his book, *The World*, which also advocated a heliocentric theory of the solar system.

René Descartes (1596-1650)

At a crucial point in his life, aiming to discover the truth in recognition of the tension between reason and religious faith, Descartes decided to start afresh, wiping clean the slate of his beliefs in a far-reaching philosophical soul-search. He proceeded by holding up all his beliefs for examination in sequence, either individually or in groups, to determine their certainty. By using a "method of doubt," he was determined to get to the bottom of things to find the truth, and upon this method, he established the basis of his philosophy.

What was this "method of doubt?" Noticing that sometimes our senses deceive us, as when we see a mirage or mistake a mosquito for a harmless gnat, and wanting to take no chances of going astray, Descartes methodically set aside beliefs based on sense perception, assuming them all to be false. This led immediately to an extreme result: as he happened to be philosophizing with this method of doubt while in his nightclothes before the fireplace in his home, he realized that he might only be having a vivid dream that he was at home in front of the fireplace.

Parenthetically, Descartes's situation of doubt in front of the fireplace has inspired some contemporary examples that convey the same idea. The first is the "brain in the vat" scenario where, unbeknownst to some person, their brain is extracted while asleep and placed into a laboratory vat, with the person continuing to have experiences as usual, except that the experiences are stimulated by electrodes. The individual presumably would not know the difference between this condition and that of regular life. Extending the thought, one can ask whether right now, we can know that we are not ourselves brains in vats, which brings us to our second example. This is shown in the movie, *The Matrix* (1999). People are put into a deep sleep, after which time electrodes are connected to their brains to stimulate ordinary-world experiences. The people do not know the difference as they remain imprisoned in their tiny cells.

Returning to Descartes, who had rethought all of his beliefs based on sense experience, and now appreciating further that he sometimes made mistakes when doing mathematical calculations, he set aside all his beliefs that involved thinking in logical sequences. To ensure completely that he did not accept any belief that might be doubted and could be false, he imagined an all-powerful "evil demon" who was trying to deceive him at every turn. This left him wondering whether there was anything at all of which he could be certain, or anything that could not be doubted, now that he found himself doubting the existence of the external world, which included his physical body, along with his logical thought processes.

At this point in his investigation, self-consciousness—Descartes's ability to think about himself—entered into the situation to save the day. He realized that although his method of doubt extended to virtually everything he knew, leaving him without any beliefs about his physical body and the surrounding world of which he could be certain, there was one thing he could not doubt: he could not doubt that he was engaged in the activity of trying to doubt everything that is possible to doubt. He realized that no matter how much he tried, he could not doubt his own existence, for whenever he tried to doubt *that*, the awareness that he was engaged in the activity of doubting confirmed to the contrary that he existed. Even an evil demon could not convince Descartes that he did not exist, for were the demon to try to convince him, that would itself confirm that Descartes existed as someone to deceive.

Descartes's method of doubt led him to conclude that "I am, I exist, is necessarily true each time that I pronounce it, or that I mentally conceive it" (Second Meditation). This is the rationale behind his famous statement, "I think, therefore I am"—in Latin, *cogito ergo sum*—that he wrote in a work entitled the *Discourse on Method* (1637). Since "*cogito*" is the Latin word for "I think," the basis of Descartes's philosophy in an act of self-consciousness is sometimes referred to as "the *cogito*." This *cogito* started a wave of modern philosophical thought whose primary focus is on the self and self-consciousness, of which Hegel's philosophy is a great descendant.

From Descartes to Kant

Between Descartes and Hegel one can cite many outstanding philosophers such as Baruch Spinoza (1632-1677), originally from Portugal who worked as a lens grinder in the Netherlands; John Locke (1632-1704), an English physician; Gottfried Wilhelm Leibniz (1646-1716), a German mathematician and diplomat; George Berkeley (1685-1753), an Irish bishop; and David Hume (1711-1776), a Scottish historian. But perhaps none was as important and influential as the German philosopher and university professor, Immanuel Kant (1724-1804), who we spoke about briefly in the previous chapter.

Like Descartes, Kant was interested in discovering what we could know for certain. He also discovered this certainty within himself, similarly to how Descartes found it in the act of self-consciousness. Rather than focusing on our self-consciousness—although this was also very important to him—Kant looked carefully at the nature of our rationality.

Immanuel Kant (1724-1804)

Impressed as well by the classical idea that human beings are essentially rational, Kant understood this to mean that humans are essentially "logical." He consequently consulted the study of formal logic to gain insight into our rational nature, for there had been a 2000-year-long history of formal logic, dating to the days of Aristotle; in its basics, not much had changed. For Kant, this stability in the study of logic was solid evidence that the patterns of thought described in his logic books provided an accurate picture of how all human beings think rationally.

One of our most basic thought processes is to be aware that a thing—it could be anything, such as a stone or a leaf—has a certain quality. When we say to ourselves "green leaf" upon perceiving a green leaf, we are employing a general logical thought pattern. To express this, we can symbolize the thing—the leaf, in our present case—with the letter "S" (for "subject") and the leaf's greenness with the letter "P" (for "property" or "predicate"). We can say in a more formula-like way, "S is P," which is a basic logical form of judgment. In a logic book, one will see this formula among the basic forms of judgment.

Kant went far with this idea, attending to 12 different forms of judgment that he found in the logic textbooks, which he understood to be the 12 basic ways in which everyone thinks rationally about themselves and the world around them. In addition to "S is P," another example is "S is not P," a negative judgment. There is also "S is necessarily P," a so-called modal judgment. Yet another example is "If A, then B," a conditional judgment, where "A" and "B" are individual propositions, as in "if one holds a flame to a piece of paper, then the paper will burn."

In Kant's 1781 book, *Critique of Pure Reason*, which he substantially revised and republished in 1787, he developed the idea that everyone organizes their experience identically in terms of the 12 basic forms of judgment. He maintained that this common style of organization explains why we all agree with each other in the fundamentals regarding the world around us—for instance, that there is a sky, a moon, a sun, trees, oceans, etc.—and why scientific theories work. Since all humans employ the same 12 forms of judgment to organize their experience, our experience is particularly "human" in this respect. And because we are rational beings, the world that we put together for ourselves according to these rules of logic, looks rational as a result.

The idea might seem obvious, but Kant drew from it some unexpected implications. Imagine how a fly experiences the world with its prismatic eyes. The fly's experience is accordingly prismatic in quality, and it is the same for all flies with such eyes. This is not because the world is itself prismatic; it is because the fly's prismatic eyes make it look that way. The fly always experiences the world through its prismatic eyes, and never experiences the world as it really is. Since all flies experience the world in the same prismatic way, they all relate to each other with the same kind of prismatic world in mind—a world that their specially-structured eyes have constructed for them. With respect to our human situation as Kant conceived of it, our position compares to that of the flies and their shared prismatic world, except that in place of the prismatic eyes, we have a set of basic logical forms.

Let us consider a second analogy to understand Kant more closely, namely, the experience of tasting some sugar with one's eyes closed. Imagine that you were "nothing but" a tongue, that some sugar crystals were placed on your surface, and that you experienced sweetness from the contact with the crystals. Now imagine that you were asked to judge from the experience of sweetness alone—this is all you have to go on—what the sugar crystals that caused the experience of sweetness look like. The question is whether from the sugar's taste alone, it is possible to infer what the sugar crystals are like in the sugar bowl on the table before being tasted, independently of one's tongue, as they are "in themselves." Needless to say, there is no way to determine anything about how the sugar crystals are in the sugar bowl, untasted, if one can judge only in reference to the experience of sweetness that the crystals cause when touching the tongue.

Kant's view of our relationship to ultimate reality, or what he calls the "thing-in-itself," is analogous. Our experience is logically structured and, Kant added, structured according to space and time which, he maintained, are nothing more than ways to organize our sensations, just like the logical forms. As such, our experience can tell us virtually nothing about how ultimate reality is in itself.

As humans, we nonetheless experience this ultimate reality in the same way, as if we were each a tongue with exactly the same structure, affected identically by whatever sugar crystals happen to come our way. We can only experience ultimate reality in our particularly human manner, namely, of individual physical things (a reflection of the "S is P" logical form), connected by cause-and-effect relationships (a reflection of the "*if* A, *then* B" logical form), in space and in time. Ultimate reality presents itself to us, we all experience how it appears in the same fundamental way, and we live together in an objective world of a certain structure. What appears to us as the objective world, however, is only an appearance, and it does not display the nature of ultimate reality as it is in itself.

Now, this might sound strange, not to mention unrealistic, since Kant seemed to have said that if I step in front of a moving horse carriage and get hit, the carriage is somehow only an "appearance" and not a real thing. It could be thought that if the carriage is merely an "appearance," then it should not have the power to do anything to us physically, since by "appearance," one usually means something like "figment of the imagination." This was not Kant's view, however. He acknowledged that there is an ultimate and objective reality that affects us—in this case, that the moving horse carriage would hurt us if we were to step in front of it—but he added that what we see as the carriage, is different from the ultimate reality that is appearing as a carriage.

Compare the situation of a worm. With regard to its sensations, a worm has a limited sense of the external world, but if it gets hit by a rock, it will squirm in pain. What it perceives as an external sensation does not represent how the rock is in itself, since its sensory system is so rudimentary. Still, the worm has a sensory experience caused by the rock, and this "appearance" can hurt it, and even kill it, even though the worm has no clear idea of what is actually hurting it. If we understand the carriage hitting us in this analogy, then we can see what it means to call the carriage an "appearance." The pleasant experience of sweetness is how the sugar crystals "appear" when they touch our tongues. The experience is an appearance of the sugar, but this does not imply that the sugar will not be nourishing to the body. Neither does referring to the carriage as an appearance suggest that nothing will happen to us if we step in front of it as it is barreling down a road.

Here is yet another way to consider the situation. Imagine, as many people do, that God is a being existing in neither space nor time. Imagine also that God does things to affect the goings-on in the physical world. Perhaps God communicates with some person with words, or appears as a fire or ghostlike apparition. None of these appearances—words, fires, apparitions—display how God is in itself, outside of space and time. The appearances are all in space and time, suited to relate to humans who live in space and time. Beyond such appearances, God remains inscrutable. The appearances would nonetheless be the real communications of God and not figments of the imagination.

Kant thought of ultimate reality, or the "thing-in-itself," and its relation to us in the same way. Ultimate reality touches us constantly, but as it truly is, it is a being that is in neither space nor time; as such, we cannot know how it is in itself. Metaphysical inquiry, understood as the investigation and description of ultimate reality as it is in itself, could therefore never succeed in Kant's view. For this reason, he is regarded as a skeptic by those who believe, to the contrary, that metaphysical inquiry is possible and that we *can* know how reality is in itself. Hegel was one of these more optimistic philosophers.

Hegel's view

Hegel was impressed with Kant's arguments—ones showing that the way we think about the world determines how the world appears to us—but he still did not believe that metaphysical knowledge is impossible. Our given perspective, however one describes it, does require us to apprehend ultimate reality through that perspective, but Hegel did not agree that this implies we can never know the absolute truth. To the contrary, he realized that we do not stand apart, or at a distance, from ultimate reality, as if we were observing a cup or a bowl of sugar on the table, or worse yet, as if we were on one side of a wall and ultimate reality were on the other side.

Hegel had a different understanding of our relationship to ultimate reality: we are rather constituted by reality, more like a fish swimming in water that is itself constituted by, or filled with, water. To understand the nature of the water within which it swims, the fish only needs to look within itself to discern what kind of substance constitutes it, for this is the same substance that constitutes its external surroundings. Similarly, since each of us is a part of reality as much as anything else is, we can look within ourselves to discover the truth of what that ultimate reality is.

This idea of being able to look within oneself successfully to discover the ultimate truth runs contrary to Kant's skepticism. It is based on the realization that we are all part of ultimate reality and that this reality flows through us as much as it flows through anything else. This insight is not specific to Hegel but is characteristic of many philosophies and religious outlooks. One can engage in meditation, for example, and aim thereby to apprehend ultimate reality, as Hinduism and Buddhism prescribe.

Although this approach to discovering the truth is promising, it is complicated by how people have different experiences when they look deeply within themselves. Some find a clear light of pure emptiness, as in Tibetan Buddhism. Some find an eternal cosmic Self, as in Hinduism. Some find the continuous flow of time, as did the French thinker, Henri Bergson (1859-1941). Some see a driving and irrational will, as in the philosophy of Hegel's contemporary, Arthur Schopenhauer (1788-1860). Yet others, as in the classical tradition that issues from the ancient Greeks, find self-consciousness and rationality, as did Hegel.

Following the path of classical Greek philosophy in conjunction with the Biblical tradition, Hegel maintained that our self-consciousness and rationality constitute the absolute, or divine aspect of us. One might suspect that his resulting metaphysical outlook would be equally traditional and straightforward. This is untrue, however, for Hegel did not conceive of God as a cosmic monarch of some sort, with a host of sub-deities who enforce moral commands, as one might find in some medieval conceptions of the heavenly world. He argued more philosophically that ultimate reality–or at least the most elementary reality (in a sense that we will later explain)–is nothing more than a network of timeless concepts without personality or consciousness. In his view, the foundation of reality is pure rationality.

For Hegel, the foundation of reality is a set of concepts, the nature and interconnection of which he described as "logic." His conception is so abstract, that if one were to expect the basis of all things to be a being with personality, explicit intelligence, and self-consciousness–i.e., "God," as usually understood–then one could easily regard Hegel's view as coming close to atheism. His metaphysics is non-traditional and radical in this regard, despite its grounding in a magnificent respect for rationality as a divine force.

Hegel had an extensively worked-out account of how the concepts that constitute the foundation of reality are related, based on the structure of self-consciousness. We will say more about this later, but for now, we can recognize that the foundation of Hegel's metaphysics is in the thoughts of rationality and self-consciousness that were at the center of the classical Greek view of the world, and as is suggested in the Bible. He was a traditional thinker, but he interpreted the traditional account in a new and innovative way.

3. Christianity and the Early Hegel

When we think of Hegel as a great philosopher, it is easy to assume from the magnitude of his achievements that he began studying and absorbing philosophical texts at an early age, just as some great musicians begin to play music as a child, as did Mozart. This was not the case for Hegel. The densely-written books through which he acquired the reputation of being a difficult and abstruse thinker appeared only after he started to teach philosophy at the University of Jena at age 30. Before this, he wrote mainly on religious themes, which he discussed straightforwardly along social, historical, and philosophical lines. That his intellectual interests and compositions were at first religiously oriented is not altogether surprising, since from an early age his family expected him to pursue an ecclesiastical vocation and educated him accordingly at a theological seminary after he graduated high school.

As mentioned in the first chapter, Hegel had written three book-length manuscripts by the time he went to Jena to work with Schelling, but had chosen not to publish them. These, along with some other essays, explored the nature of Christianity and were written in a clear, approachable style. One of his earliest essays was "On the Prospects for a Folk Religion" (1793), also called the "Tübingen Fragment" or the "Tübingen Essay," written when he was completing his theological studies, just prior to assuming his position as a tutor in Bern. He was approaching his 23rd birthday at the time.

Hegel then accepted Kant's moral theory—a theory that determines moral principles through pure reason—but his more pragmatic and worldly orientation left him frustrated with Kant's view, for he wondered how to inform people's lives with a theory that, at first sight, appeared to be too abstract and remote. Hegel believed that the practical task of rendering abstract moral imperatives into easily understandable ideas is one of religion's main social functions, for he saw how Christianity promoted moral awareness by introducing the respected image of God as the supreme moral authority and law-giver.

In his Tübingen essay, Hegel speaks disapprovingly of abstract, pure moral philosophy considered in isolation, referring to it with terms such as "cold understanding," "cold cognitions," and "cold conviction." It is not, though, as if he rejected the substance of Kant's moral theory. It was fine as far as it went, but it stood for him as an abstract framework in need of a concrete cultural application. It was like a well-formed skeleton that required some organs, muscles, and flesh to be able to live and move.

Convinced that religion is more than a voluminous and authoritative listing of moral rules and regulations, Hegel maintained that it is most importantly a matter of the heart. He wrote that the heart speaks louder than the abstract understanding, and that to live in a genuinely moral way, we need to develop our feelings.

Here, his model and inspiration was the folk religion of the ancient Greeks. For many of Hegel's generation, Greek society stood as a cultural ideal, for it appeared to have been filled with well-balanced people who successfully blended their abstract moral codes with an enthusiastic passion that was felt throughout the population. Hegel spoke of the cheerfulness of the Greeks in contrast to the dour atmosphere he found in the churches of his day, hoping that in his own society, a spirit as equally inspirational as the Greeks' could come alive.

The Acropolis in Athens with the Parthenon (447-432 BCE), a symbol of ancient Greece

When Hegel moved from Tübingen to Bern, his project of fostering the resurgence of the Greek spirit receded into the background while he investigated some of the specific difficulties involved with Christianity, like a doctor diagnosing a patient. His advocacy of Kant's moral theory consequently moved into the foreground as the foundation of his inquiries. As interested as he was to render abstract moral principles concrete, he remained captivated by the idea that all religions are essentially the same in their moral content. He believed that Kant's moral theory expressed this content well, and that the manifest differences in religions are the source of misunderstanding and needless conflict.

Hegel complemented his interest in "concreteness," where he accentuated the importance of human feeling, with an interest in "universality"–a theme inherent in the views of the French revolutionaries. The revolutionaries spoke not merely of Frenchmen, but of humanity as a whole, hoping that everyone would someday be able to achieve their freedom. In the spirit of Enlightenment, Kant also wrote for humanity, and not exclusively or primarily for Germans.

With this universalistic inspiration, Hegel wrote *Life of Jesus*, characterizing Jesus as an embodiment and expression of the principles of Kant's moral theory—a theory that speaks to all people—as if Jesus were the voice of the highest humanity. Completing the other side of the picture, in *The Positivity of the Christian Religion*, Hegel interpreted the accidental, non-essential, and rhetorical aspects of Christianity—aspects such as rituals and accounts of Jesus's miracles—merely as useful vehicles to help convey Christianity's essential moral message.

The word "positivity" appears in the book's title, signifying "that which is of secondary value." As Hegel applied it to Christianity, the word refers to non-essential, historically derived, and often authoritarian aspects of the religion; together, they contrast with its "natural," essential, moral, and freedom-nurturing quality. The "positivity" of Christianity refers to features of the religion that either obscure, or have mistakenly taken the place of, its essential moral message.

Hegel adopted the terms "positive" and "natural" from legal theory, where they indicate the difference between imperfect, human-written, secondary, "positive" law, and perfect, primary, God-given, "natural" law. If one is a legislator, the ideal legal practice would be to enact positive laws that match up with what are regarded as the actual, true, and morally-grounded laws that God comprehends. Among its variety of meanings, the phrase in the Lord's Prayer, "thy will be done on earth as it is in heaven," can be understood as a moral-legal directive to construct and to live in view of laws whose intentions are not merely pragmatic, but are also moral.

Of love and people

Hegel remained in Bern as a house tutor for three years, from 1793 until 1796. When he left Bern for Frankfurt, he still advocated Kant's moral theory in the spirit of the French Revolution and the Enlightenment, and viewed Jesus primarily as the voice of universal reason. He was not yet gravitating into the detailed study of human history to discern the reason we are here, as he would in later years. He was more simply appreciating the unity of religions and the unity of all people in terms of the timeless principles they share. These principles are universal, comparable to 2+2=4 or any other mathematical truth, and they hold steadfastly throughout changes in history, location, and time.

Upon his move to Frankfurt, Hegel's renewed contact with his friend, Friedrich Hölderlin, whose influence refreshed his interest in accentuating feeling as the spiritual core of religion and led him to promote love as the central religious feeling. We see this in Hegel's 1798-99 book, *The Spirit of Christianity*, as well as in a short text from 1797 or early 1798 referred to as his "Fragment on Love." Hegel departed from Kant in these writings, describing love as a superior feeling that transcends all duties and stands beyond abstract moral rules.

He believed that when love is present—for instance, parents' love for their children—helping out, caring for their loved ones, giving advice, telling the truth, keeping promises, offering protection, showing them respect, setting good examples, and so on, are not done as a matter of "duty." Rather, they issue from a pure, selfless, and tender spirit. Realizing this, Hegel was convinced that when people are united through feelings of love, the kind of unity achieved is more substantial than that which arises from recognizing our common logical capacities and moral rules, as Kant held.

The situation compares with respect to God. When acting morally out of love for God, one does not act slavishly out of sheer obedience or fear of God's power, authority, or threat of damnation. The motivation is holy, beautiful, and perhaps thankful. Following this more romantic path, Hegel distanced himself from the legalistic, "rule-book" conception of religion and morality, encouraging a more heartfelt attitude that yields a genuine sense of community.

In his "Fragment on Love," Hegel observed that as an effective unifying principle, love creates a feeling of equality between people. When love is mutual, neither person is "dead" to the other, for, he said, each regards the other as a living being from every point of view. In contrast, when one unlovingly uses another person as a mere means to an end, the person is being treated more like an inanimate, subordinate object, and less like a living, equally respectable being.

This insistence on respecting everyone cohered perfectly with Kant's moral theory, for Kant also prescribed treating people with common respect and dignity, and never using them solely for selfish reasons, as if they were mere tools. The difference between the two philosophers is that Hegel believed that love achieves these moral ends in a more concrete, heartfelt way. The implied criticism of Kant—one familiar during Hegel's time—is that Kant's moral theory is too calculating and distant, both emotionally and physically, and needs to be enhanced with an emphasis upon feelings over abstract understanding.

Kant's contemporary Friedrich Schiller had maintained as well that Kant too sharply divorced reason from sensation, and that reason and sensation should be in harmony for a person to act with the right moral motivation. Some years later, when Hegel was a professor in Berlin during the 1820s, Arthur Schopenhauer—then a young philosopher and Hegel's colleague—objected to Kant's moral theory on the same grounds, claiming that it is too intellectualized, and that the true basis of morality is the feeling of compassion.

For unifying people, Hegel now regarded love as preferable to abstract reasoning, for love achieves this unity without passing over each person's individuality. Abstract Kantian moral principles less

In his Tübingen essay some years before, he spoke of "wisdom" as opposed to "rationalization," where by "rationalization" he meant formal, logical, or abstract reasoning. Prior to the composition of the Oldest System fragment, he had perceived, if only dimly at first, that standard formal logic is not the most profound and philosophically central form of rationality, and that there is a higher sense of reason to consider.

The Oldest System document was written in 1796, Hegel's fragment on love in 1797, and his book, *The Spirit of Christianity*, was finished in 1799. Let us now look at some of Hegel's writings in 1800, immediately before he moved to Jena in January 1801, for his thought underwent an important transition at this time.

Hegel in the new decade

Following his tendency to understand the subjects about which he wrote with greater concreteness, Hegel revised *The Positivity of the Christian Religion* in 1800. Although he did not go much further than rewriting the book's preface, there was a change in his perspective that can be seen in his use of the words "positive" and "natural." In the original 1795 manuscript, he used the word "positive" to refer to Christianity's unnecessary historical details, accidents, and contingencies, usually with a disapproving suggestion of authoritarianism and mindless rule-following. These "positive" aspects of Christianity contrasted with abstract, essential, timeless truths, which Hegel referred to as "natural" in the sense of God-given "natural law."

We can refer to Hegel's 1795 usage as the "enlightenment" version of the distinction between "positive" and "natural." He accordingly described Jesus's miracles, not as "miracles" in the metaphysical sense, but merely as ways to create an attractive social avenue for people to attend to his main moral message, using his medical knowledge impressively and authoritatively to cure some people whose illness had brought them to the edge of death. This "positive" versus "natural" distinction provided Hegel with a useful way to formulate criticisms of those who were too attached to rituals and worldly religious regulations, as one might find in dietary restrictions, designated holy days and places, calendar arrangements, prescribed bodily posturing, and clothing requirements.

In 1800, Hegel revised his understanding of the distinction between "positive" and "natural" after having realized that although certain attitudes may seem false and misguided to us *today*, they were appropriate and reasonable for the time in which they originated. For instance, there had been rules in various communities for prohibiting the consumption of certain animals, often for either economic or health reasons. Given the social conditions at the time, the rules made sense. However, after long-term historical changes in social structure, technology (e.g., refrigerators), food availability, ways of earning a living, prevailing values and such, the prohibitions became more questionable, since the original context in which they arose carried a practical meaning that had essentially disappeared. There are many examples like this. It is like growing up: when one is young, certain activities are fun and engaging, such as playing with toy soldiers or dolls; when one grows older, a more mature perspective renders the childhood activities less captivating.

Hegel accordingly revised his use of the word "natural," changing it from "timeless essence," to the more historically-attentive "that which accords with the spirit of the times." The word "positive" correspondingly assumed the meaning of "anachronistic," or out of sync with the spirit of the times. The general prescription to "be natural," we should add, remained throughout this change.

This shift in meaning may seem minor, but it indicates a significant development in Hegel's outlook. When faced with a set of timeless truths in isolation, he was always disposed to give them some concrete application. His first style of achieving this was through an emphasis upon subjective religious feeling, and although it had its advantages, it did not take the flow of history into substantial account. As a religious feeling, love is an immediate matter within a real-life context, without any particular consideration of the wider context of human history.

Hegel always seemed to recognize that there is no such thing as a "human" in the abstract, since people are not mere thoughts, definitions, or empty conceptual forms; they are physical beings with a determinate size and shape, weight, age, eyes of a certain color, number of hairs on the skin, and so on. His strong sense of being down-to-earth and emphasis on feeling, though, did not at first take account of our involvement in "world history" per se. He attended closely to physical details and immediate feelings in his initial effort to think realistically, but he did not incorporate them into the wider perspective of long-term historical change.

Around the year 1800, however, Hegel began to appreciate human history more explicitly as a growth process in which we are all participating. There are different cultures and civilizations at different times with different values, and these values are appropriate and natural to the various times and places. Civilization and cultures develop, and when this happens, values transform, sometimes radically, and what used to be natural, automatic, or uncritically assumed, soon becomes unnatural. Five hundred years ago, no one was understanding human knowledge in terms of computers and computability, since there were no computers. Three thousand years ago, no one was understanding moral action in terms of what Jesus said, since Jesus had not yet been born and Christianity did not exist.

With the introduction of the idea of historical development, as well as awareness that wars, hard work, and terrible suffering often accompany major historical changes, a new image of Jesus emerged to influence Hegel's writing and thinking. Having started with a rationalistic, "enlightenment" conception of Jesus as the spokesperson for Kantian moral theory, and then having moved into a romantic conception of Jesus as the preacher of universal love, Hegel now thought more historically and developmentally of

Jesus as a suffering individual who carried a heavy cross on a way of despair, ascending the hill to his crucifixion, but also to his glorification. This became his new model for understanding people and the world—a model of growth and development that features labor, suffering, and struggle as necessary means to reach a most valuable goal.

With this distinctively historical and developmental orientation, Hegel's style of thought also became more encyclopedic, for to speak intelligently about whether human history has a fundamental meaning and direction requires extensive knowledge of humanity's collective experience. The themes of growth, development, labor, and the quest for the widest comprehension were now to predominate in Hegel's thought, as he understood the ultimate truth to reside in "the whole" of everything.

Hegel's Three Conceptions of Jesus: (1) The Enlightenment Jesus (1793-95) Jesus as the Preacher of Kant's Moral Theory (2) The Romantic Jesus (1796-99) Jesus as the Embodiment of Love (3) Jesus as the Image of Historical Development (1800-31) Jesus as the Suffering Cross-Bearer

4. *The Phenomenology of Spirit* I: The Truth is the Whole

H egel's *Phenomenology of Spirit* is among the most influential books in the history of Western philosophy, rich in ideas and filled with insights. There is an often-recited story about the book's completion in October 1806 when Hegel and Napoleon happened to cross paths. Just as Hegel was finishing the book, Napoleon was approaching Jena, the city in which Hegel was living, aiming to fight the Prussian army. On the day Napoleon arrived, Hegel watched him riding out of the city on horseback to do some reconnaissance before the battle, impressed by the Emperor's commanding presence. Hegel had recently been theorizing about world history on a broad scale in the *Phenomenology*, so the experience was especially memorable. On that day—a traumatic one for the citizens of Jena, with the French soldiers entering and occupying the city—Hegel wrote to his friend Friedrich Niethammer that he had seen the Emperor, "this world soul" (*Weltseele*), in person.

After Napoleon's victory against the Prussians on the following day, some French soldiers ransacked Hegel's apartment, where the last few sheets of the *Phenomenology* were kept. Fortunately, Hegel had already sent off the bulk of the book's concluding segments to the publishers at the end of the preceding week, so the bulk of his work was safe. Throughout the battle, though, he remained worried about losing the manuscript's final segments in the mail amidst the chaos. At the time, he was a relatively obscure, financially-needy university lecturer trying to make a name for himself with his new book. Unbeknownst to everyone, his influence on the world of philosophy would grow.

The Battle of Jena, October 14, 1806

The Introduction to the *Phenomenology*

The *Phenomenology* begins with a long Preface followed by a shorter Introduction. The Preface explains the work's basic philosophical method, which we will describe below. The Introduction specifically clears the philosophical ground for the book's ascent to absolute knowledge by challenging Kant's views. Hegel argued against Kant's skeptical, project-threatening claim that absolute knowledge is impossible to achieve, given how our particularly human way of knowing things unavoidably introduces a distortive and limiting factor into whatever we know. We described this Kantian position in Chapter 2.

To recall, in Hegel's view Kant was mistaken to assume that we are separated at a distance from "reality" or "the truth," as if our reason were like a telescope used to perceive distant objects, and as if "the truth" were like some distant object that we can see only through the telescope and never directly touch. Hegel maintained that this model is incorrect and misleading: since we are each a part of reality as much as anything else, ultimate reality, or the truth, flows through us from the very start, and in a sense, "is" us. We embody the truth ourselves, so the truth is not at a distance.

What we want ultimately to know, then, is something that we already are. The problem of human knowledge is not that we are sharply separated from reality or the truth, and need to bridge a gap, or span a distance, to encounter it face-to-face. Rather, it is that our ordinary state of knowledge is cloudy, and does not allow us immediately to apprehend clearly the reality that we already, intrinsically, and constitutively are.

Accordingly, Hegel's philosophical task in the Phenomenology was to clarify our awareness of who and what we are, to achieve a more explicit awareness of ultimate reality as a matter of self-knowledge. In principle, his method is straightforward: since we are already constituted by the reality we seek to know, every perspective in which we might find ourselves, no matter how limited it might be, has a grain of truth already built into it. Whether our perspective is simple or comprehensive, all we need to do—although this is not necessarily easy or quick—is to work through that perspective until it breaks down of its own accord and gives way to a more comprehensive view, and to repeat that process until we arrive at a totally comprehensive perspective. Since "the truth" is everything that there is, the goal of knowledge is to achieve total knowledge by advancing step-by-step into increasingly comprehensive perspectives, like a person who develops to maturity and eventually sees the world in a more knowledgeable light.

Working through a given perspective is not an automatic, rapid, or easy matter. We must live through it sufficiently to exhaust its content, so it can break down naturally into a more mature outlook. For certain individuals, it could take years to grow beyond a particular mindset. Imagine a person who loves to make money, either for buying bigger and better things, or simply for the sake of watching a bank account balance continually climb. We have all heard stories of people who materially "have everything," but who nonetheless feel empty inside. The same tends to be true at the heights of fame. As the perspective plays itself out and emptiness arises, there is a change in interests, values, and outlook. For some, it may take decades to move into a new perspective, and many die before experience has accumulated sufficiently to precipitate the perspective's breakdown. Nonetheless, every perspective has a natural limit that, when reached, opens the door to a new outlook. It is only a matter of time and accumulated experience. For Hegel, the absolute perspective awaits at the end, which includes everything. Since the absolute perspective is totally inclusive, he stated that the truth "is the whole."

The universe is here conceived as a single growth process that encompasses everything, as if it were an oak that is growing from an acorn into a tall, strong, leafy tree, and as if each of us were presently a part of, and participant in, that growing tree. Hegel applied this developmental vision to each subject upon which he reflected, understanding it dynamically as engaged in a growth process. This is not the usual way of considering things, since the normal tendency is to attend more narrowly and immediately to what is happening in the present moment, as we walk down the street, go shopping, talk to friends, and such, assuming that the objects we perceive are mostly static and self-contained, as we might pick up a cup to take a drink, imagining the cup to be nothing more than the solid object that we hold in our hand.

The Preface to the *Phenomenology*

In this section—a lengthy overview that Hegel wrote after the book was completed, unlike the relatively brief Introduction, which he wrote at the project's beginning—Hegel set forth his leading idea and inspiration for his philosophical method, positing that everything that is participating in a universal growth process. Accordingly, if one wants to understand something—let's use the example of a bird—it is an error to believe that "the bird" is nothing more than the animal that happens to be flying overhead. In greater depth beyond the present moment, the bird has a history, for it grew into the condition that we presently observe. To know the bird well, we need to include an awareness of its past.

The bird's growth process can't be considered independently either, detaching it from the bird we see above us. The present physical bird is the result of the growth process to date, connected to and integrated within that process. Moreover, neither is "the bird" the abstract idea, definition, anatomical plan, or essence of the individual bird that we presently observe. By itself, the bird's "essence," or "kind," or "form," lacks physical feathers, a beak, wings, and a beating heart, for the bird's form is merely an abstraction, and is not a living organism. To understand the bird flying above us, we need to integrate all three: (1) our idea of the bird's essence or kind, (2) the specific process over time through which the bird grew up, and (3) the physical bird as we perceive it at this moment, as the product of that process. The essence, the process, and the product, as a blended unity, together constitute the truth of the situation and of the bird we observe.

[Plan → Development → Product]
[← **T r u e r   U n d e r s t a n d i n g** →]

Hegel applied this developmental, life-oriented outlook–one that pertains immediately to living things–to everything that is. Consider the field of study known as "philosophy." For any philosophy to which we might refer, Hegel initially considered its place in the long and complicated history of philosophical thought. Following this idea, suppose we then locate a given philosophy in its historical place, setting Plato's philosophy (c. 380 B.C.E.) between the Pre-Socratic philosophers (c. 600-400 B.C.E.) and Aristotle (c. 330 B.C.E.). This is a reasonable start, but a danger now arises. Hegel warned against assuming that a given "later" philosophy always stands as the refutation of an "earlier" one, in the sense that the earlier philosophy, as historically superseded, can now be thrown away and disregarded. We should add that this need not be a philosophy per se. It could be a religion, or kind of political system, or style of moral evaluation, that occurred in the past, for Hegel's point is a general one about how to regard historical phenomena.

To flatly reject some earlier historical phenomenon in favor of a later one is misguided in Hegel's view, for it overlooks how historical change is an integrated process. In our example, Hegel conceived of each philosophy (or religion, etc.) as a phase of "philosophical thought," regarded as a single, developing entity. He saw "philosophical thought," or "philosophy" with a capital "P," as if it were a growing plant, where the early philosophies are the "buds," the subsequent philosophies are the "blossoms," and the contemporary ones are the "fruits." His point was that without the buds and blossoms, there could be no fruits, and all three aspects are of the very same plant. They are moments of a single process that is the plant, understood historically and dynamically. We can understand people in the same way: we all have a history that informs what and who we are today; to understand ourselves, we must therefore understand our history.

Hegel used this "bud-blossom-fruit" image in the Preface to the *Phenomenology*, but the image of a caterpillar morphing into a butterfly is also apt, since metamorphosis more explicitly captures the idea of how the successive perspectives that knowledge assumes in the *Phenomenology* often radically improve upon their predecessors, to the point where the world looks completely different as a result. Think of how we can know a cup in immediate perception as a solid material object, and then scientifically, as a dynamic aggregate of invisible atoms that renders the cup into mostly empty space.

We should also note that the images of living things that Hegel used to illustrate his style of thought work only up to a point, since he described the development of knowledge as culminating with complete and absolute comprehension, without any subsequent degeneration or death, even though death is also an essential aspect of living organisms. When using analogies, it is important to remember that every analogy has its limits.

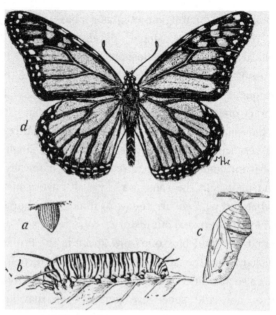

The Stages of a Butterfly's Development

In accord with his developmental style of thinking, Hegel criticized the "either/or," (or "on/off," "plus/minus," or "true/false") exclusionary style of thought. Within this mode, either a given philosophical outlook is entirely accepted, or it is entirely rejected. Either a given religion is entirely accepted, or it is entirely rejected, and so on, for any given subject matter and situation. In Hegel's judgment, to think in terms of this exclusionary style is one-sided and not well-suited for understanding the whole truth. The spirit of Hegel's philosophy is inclusive and reconciliatory, and it does not reject anything. For instance, he located even the "either/or" style of thought, which he called "understanding," as a less mature phase in the development of logic, where it stands as a predecessor to the more inclusive, process-oriented, reconciliatory style he called "reason." In non-superficial contexts, Hegel did not speak of something being "simply true" or "simply false," but rather of it being "less true" or "more true," conceiving of truth as a matter of degree, intensity, and comprehensiveness.

Associated with Hegel's concept of reason and historical development is a prescription for proper education. To be educated well in some subject is to understand the history of that subject, and to see oneself as a product of that history. If one is a musician, then one would study the history of music to understand what one is playing. If one is a philosopher, then one would study the history of philosophy, and regard one's own thoughts as a product and aspect of that history. It is insufficient and not well-educated to attend only to contemporary styles and fashions, setting aside the works of the past as unimportant. Not only is it true that those who cannot remember the past are condemned to repeat it, as was stated by the philosopher George Santayana (1863-1952), but if one does not study history, one fails to understand oneself.

We have been speaking generally about Hegel's style of thinking, which regards everything as developing and growing like a living organism. The *Phenomenology of Spirit* is itself a prime example of this style, as it focusses specifically upon the nature and growth of human knowledge. Just as one can consider any given philosophy as a moment or aspect of the development of "philosophical thought" or of "Philosophy"—as if philosophy itself were a single, living entity that grows to maturity over time—one can also consider different ways of knowing as moments or aspects of the development of "Knowledge," as if it were also a single, living entity that grows to maturity over time. More informally, one can say that "Knowledge" is the main character of Hegel's *Phenomenology of Spirit*—a book that allows us to experience its long journey to maturity.

During Hegel's time, there was a popular literary genre called the "educational novel" or *Bildungsroman* (in German, "*Bildung*" means "education" or "formation," and "*Roman*" means "novel") wherein the novel's main character develops and comes of age through a series of challenges. One of the best-known is Goethe's *Wilhelm Meister's Apprenticeship* (1795-96), published when Hegel was concluding his tutoring job in Bern, just before his move to Frankfurt. In more recent times, examples include James Joyce's *A Portrait of the Artist as a Young Man* (1916), Herman Hesse's *Siddhartha* (1922), and Margaret Mitchell's *Gone with the Wind* (1936).

This idea of a *Bildungsroman* inspired the American philosopher, Josiah Royce, (1855-1916) citing Goethe's novel in his 1906 lectures on modern idealism, to describe Hegel's *Phenomenology* as "a biography of the world spirit." One can also describe the *Phenomenology* as the *Bildungsroman* of "Knowledge" in a personified sense, since the book works through knowledge's "coming of age," beginning, as it does, with the most elementary forms of knowledge and progressing to the most comprehensive.

Three main parts

As we see in its table of contents, *Phenomenology* divides into three main parts, entitled "Consciousness," "Self-consciousness," and a third, untitled part comprised of four segments that define an explicitly rational orientation towards the world. Each of the book's main parts describes a series of different perspectives or "shapes of consciousness" that knowledge assumes.

In the first stage, knowledge attends—as one would naturally do and expect—to immediately surrounding objects, and develops in a series of phases that keeps ordinary objects constantly in view. It starts specifically with our initial, commonsense perception of inanimate objects such as cups, trees, rocks, lamps, and chairs, and develops into the sophisticated scientific knowledge of those objects. Knowledge's fundamental attitude within this first stage shows a basic confidence in sensory experience. The different shapes of consciousness are all "object-oriented" in this part of the book, which Hegel entitled, "Consciousness," having in mind our direct, unreflective, and immediately engaged awareness of ordinary objects.

After exhausting its knowledge of external material objects by coming to know them thoroughly in a scientific way (we will describe how this occurs in the next chapter), the journey of knowledge moves to the second of the book's three main parts. The knowing consciousness now reverses the direction of its attention and turns inward—it turns towards itself in an act of reflection, thinking about what it has been doing—and becomes explicitly aware of itself as a self-conscious individual.

When subsequently looking outward, the knowing consciousness no longer regards what it knows as merely inanimate objects, but recognizes in them, as a reflection of itself, the presence of other people—a presence absent in the earlier phases of knowledge in the first part of the book. Other people now appear within the various, forms of knowledge that unfold. These shapes of consciousness begin with an extremely selfish outlook, hostile towards other people, developing gradually into less selfish forms. An attitude of self-centeredness nonetheless persists throughout this second part, and Hegel entitled this section of the book, "self-consciousness," in accord with its "self-oriented" or "subject-oriented" set of outlooks.

After exhausting the set of self-centered ways of knowing, knowledge attains a more balanced, non-selfish, positively social condition where other people appear as equals in principle. This introduces a series of outlooks that involve morality, culture, and the feeling of being at home in the world. Again, as he had done throughout the book, Hegel ordered these outlooks from the more elementary and abstract to the more complicated and down-to-earth. This third and final part of the *Phenomenology* is characterized throughout by a "rational-certainty" that divides into four sub-sections: "reason," "spirit," "religion," and "Absolute Knowledge."

The culmination of the journey is absolute knowledge—a condition that permits one to speak metaphysically about the ultimate nature of things and to develop those thoughts into a system, or what Hegel called a "science." In this respect, *Phenomenology* serves as the introduction to, and justification for, the philosophical system that he composed thereafter, beginning with the *Science of Logic*. This explains the book's published title, *System of Science, by Ge. Wilh. Fr. Hegel, First Part, The Phenomenology of Spirit*.

We should mention that the word "spirit," as it appears in the book's English title, "*Phenomenology of Spirit*," is the translation of the German word "*Geist*" in the German title, *Phänomenologie des Geistes*. An early English translation of the *Phenomenology* by James Black Baillie in 1910 translated "*Geist*" as "mind," so sometimes one sees Hegel's book referred to as the *Phenomenology of Mind*.

Settling upon "spirit" or "mind" as the translation of "*Geist*" is difficult, since the word has both meanings. The best way to understand the word as it appears in the *Phenomenology* is to refer to Hegel's own statement regarding its meaning, which is neither "spirit" nor "mind" in the ordinary sense. By the word *Geist*, he meant harmonious social consciousness, reminiscent of the folk religion and integrated social spirit that he found so attractive in ancient Greek society when he was a theology student in Tübingen.

Hegel characterized *Geist* as the "I" that is "we," and the "we" that is "I." Superficially considered, this is the idea of a contented group consciousness, where one feels connected to a group, while still feeling respected as an individual, as when one is at an animated and friendly party, or sports event for one's home team, or religious service in a religion that one believes in. More profoundly considered, it conveys the idea of a perfect society—all for one and one for all, with everyone acting morally and working together for the common good. *Geist* expresses a communal consciousness in the best sense of the word, a "commune," where people share their belongings and work well together. Hegel's ultimate vision of the world was as a great commune, where everyone worked together.

5. *The Phenomenology of Spirit* II: The Ascent to Absolute Knowledge

I f we look for straightforward examples of what we "know," it is tempting to say that the objects we perceive directly in front of us are things that we know. I might say in a self-evident fashion, "here is one hand" and "here is another," following the example of the English philosopher G. E. Moore (1873-1958) in his 1939 essay "Proof of an External World." Or I might repeat the words of Descartes, "here I am, sitting in front of the fireplace, thinking about philosophy."

Although it did not take long for Descartes to wonder whether he was in fact sitting in front of the fireplace, speculating in the extreme that he could instead be having a vivid dream, we ordinarily trust our perceptions and believe that they tell us accurately that the objects we see before us have a reality of their own. Were we to lose consciousness, we would do so assuming implicitly that those objects will be there when we regain consciousness. We assume this when we go to sleep each night, expecting to wake up to the world basically as we left it, to resume our activities in continuity with the previous day. It is easy to conclude from this that the simplest objects that we know are the tables, chairs, trees, beds, and fireplaces that we directly and immediately perceive.

Hegel begins his *Phenomenology* with this state of mind, in a form of knowledge that he called "immediate knowledge" or "sense certainty." It is immediate, simple, refers to individuals, and is the natural place to start an investigation of knowledge. Here, in the beginning, Hegel supposed that we do not heavily interpret the objects we perceive, but take them indirectly, just as they are. Just as Descartes started his *Meditations*, Hegel too began the

Phenomenology and his own investigation of knowledge by attending in an ordinary manner to the objects that surround us in our daily lives.

The first question Hegel asked was whether this kind of knowledge is truly "immediate," "simple," and appropriate as the starting point for the *Phenomenology*, for he wanted to begin with the most elementary form of knowledge. Like Descartes, he noticed a problem: the commonsense perceptual situation is not as simple and immediate as it first appears. Therefore, if we intend philosophically to begin with "immediate knowledge" in its true form, then it is necessary to reconsider the ordinary perceptual situation in which we find ourselves.

If an object is "simple," then it cannot have any parts, so we must ask what kinds of objects these could possibly be. Tables, chairs, and trees have parts. Also, if an object is known "immediately," then it must be considered entirely on its own, and not in any relationship to other things. Using Hegelian phrasing, our knowledge of the simple object cannot be "mediated" by references to other things. "Immediate knowledge," then, cannot be of a complex object such as a table, chair, or tree; it must rather be of a simple item considered singly, in isolation from its surroundings.

It follows that the object of immediate knowledge is not some ordinary perceptual object, which is complex, but something more basic—say, an infinitesimal point in space, "right here," or infinitesimal point in time, "right now." Appreciating the need for an elementary beginning, Hegel revised his original starting point to begin the *Phenomenology* with a more accurate conception of immediate knowledge—one from which other, more complicated forms of knowledge can emerge. He consequently started with the knowledge of an atomistic, empty point in space or in time that is right here, or right now. For Hegel, the knowledge of such a point would be "immediate knowledge" in its true form. It is not rich in content, with a wealth of overflowing colors and shapes. Rather, it is the thinnest in content, and refers to nothing more than an infinitesimal point.

To experience immediate knowledge, Hegel considered what it is to know a single moment, or what can be called the "punctual present." He asks to "point" to it. When we do, though, something unexpected happens: when we point to "right now," that present moment immediately disappears into the past and is replaced by a new moment that counts as "right now." The moment we point to as "right now" immediately becomes "not now" as we pass into a later point in time. This happens constantly: the initial moment is replaced by a new moment, different from the moment to which we initially point.

As we reflect upon this activity and try to hold the "present" in mind, we automatically expand our conception of "the present" to encompass more than the punctual present. We think more broadly of a time span of a few seconds, realizing that this is how we need to conceive of "right now" to comprehend the situation. The punctual "right now" passes into "not now" as we point to it, and then upon reflection, the moments are thought of together in a more extensive notion of "right now," considered as a short time span.

Now   Not-Now   Synthesis of Now/Not-Now
                                              (i.e., a time-span)

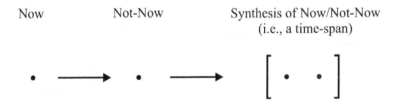

The structure of the time span at which we have arrived can be represented generally as a pair of brackets containing a set of points: {........}. This is what we now "know," having passed from a condition of immediate knowledge to a more complicated mode where the object of our knowledge is not a single point, but a time span. We can describe this single time span as a "one" that has many points within it. The time span has the structure of a "one" that contains a "many."

An important aspect of this structure is that in its abstract form, it is also the basic structure of any ordinary perceptual object, which we can describe as a single thing (a "one") with a variety of properties (a "many"). We perceive a cup of coffee that has a variety of colors, shapes, odors, textures, and so on. From the apprehension of a single point, then, we have moved to the awareness of a time span, and from the structure of the time span, we have before us the core structure of any perceptual object. This marks a development from "immediate knowledge" to a new, more complicated state of awareness, namely, "perception." It is here, in perception, where our ordinary awareness of objects such as tables and chairs has its proper place.

Inherent in the perceptual object is a tension between its singularity as a "table" or "chair," and its multiplicity insofar as it has many different properties. One way to comprehend this tension is to say that the object has an essence that defines its stable, true, aspect or "oneness," and a set of variable properties that can change without affecting the object's integrity. We can paint the table a different color, for example, and yet speak of it as the same table, having in mind the kind of thing it is that has remained the same.

If we think further about the object as a thing of a certain kind (say, a table), we do, however, implicitly contrast that kind of object with other kinds of objects. A table is not a chair, or a lamp, or a clock, etc. Also, if we perceive the table in front of us in a realistic way, as opposed to thinking of it independently of its surroundings in a more abstract manner, we perceive it against a background of other objects. The table is in a room, set upon a floor, surrounded by pictures on the walls, next to a doorway, perhaps in front of some windows, and so on, all of which we apprehend jointly as a set of interrelated items. We are no longer thinking about the table, or chair, or door as individual and independent items, but about the whole room that contains many objects. Stated more generally, we are attending to our entire perceptual field, where each object is set off by, and set against, the other objects in the room.

This brings us to a more dynamic awareness where our knowledge is about a set of interconnected objects. As we reflect even further, the relationships between the objects become salient, and our awareness transforms from being aware of a set of static objects, to becoming aware of the relationships, or "forces" that hold among those objects. We appreciate how our body is reflected in a mirror, how the weight of the table makes an impression on the rug, how the heat of the coffee cup warms the air around it, and eventually, how the objects we perceive are energetically related to each other as a single field of interacting forces. Our perception is now attuned to a field of energy that assumes a variety of forms, such as tables, chairs, windows, mirrors, and such, and is starting to have a more scientific aspect.

Knowledge has progressed from a single point to a time span, to a perceptual object, to the field of perception regarded as a set of static perceptual objects, to the field of perception regarded as a constantly changing array of energy patterns. Our knowledge has developed from a single static point to a comprehensive and dynamic field of energy, growing step-by-step, like a plant.

To "know" something involves appreciating the "truth" of that which we know, and truth—if we follow Plato's insight about the nature of truth—is something that is permanent. Grasping at smoke that escapes our fingers is less true than holding onto a rock, and mathematical truths such as 2+2=4 are more permanent than any rock or mountain range. To understand the truth of the perceptual field conceived of as a constantly fluctuating field of energy, we need to discern some permanence in that fluctuating field. This can be done by finding some basic patterns that underlie the energy field's changes, expressible mathematically as natural laws.

The upshot is a new, two-level structure for knowledge: there is the perceptual *appearance*, which is constantly fluctuating and therefore difficult to comprehend, and there is also the underlying, non-perceptual, conceptual *reality*, expressed by the laws of nature, which is true and stable, at least at first. The "appearance vs. reality" distinction now emerges as a ground for the scientific form of knowledge.

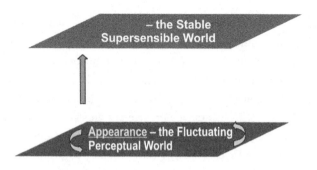

As we learn more about the perceptual field and develop our scientific knowledge, our understanding of the laws of nature becomes increasingly comprehensive and specific. The initially tranquil realm of laws that contrasts with the changing perceptual field becomes more detailed, more complex, and more encompassing of the changes that occur in the perceptual field. If we push this process to the end—although in fact, scientific knowledge in our present-day world has not yet reached this level of explanation, and probably never will, for we speak now of an ideal—then every change in the perceptual world will be explained, understood, and virtually *replicated* in our scientific understanding of the world.

The endpoint is a complete replication of the perceptual field in our understanding, operating as dynamically as does the perceptual world itself. In that state of knowledge, everything in the perceptual field is known and explained thoroughly.

With the attainment of complete, seamless scientific knowledge, the first stage of knowledge, which Hegel refers to under the title, "consciousness"—the movement from immediate knowledge, to perception, to scientific understanding—is completed. From the standpoint of idealized scientific knowledge, the perception of any object is of something that has been thoroughly understood and reconstructed in the understanding. The object's presentation is no longer foreign, for having been reconstructed in the understanding, it has become a reflection of oneself. One sees "oneself," i.e., one knows a product of one's own scientific understanding, when one perceives the object. From this state of knowledge emerges the next main stage, which Hegel refers to as "self-consciousness."

Self-consciousness

One thing to notice in the various forms of knowledge that arise in the initial, "consciousness" segment of the *Phenomenology*, is that there are no people involved. The objects of awareness are inanimate, such as points, time-spans, ordinary perceptual objects like tables and chairs, energy fields, and scientific laws. We are moving now into a different level of knowledge that is more practical and, most importantly, social. Beginning once again with the simplest version of this kind of knowledge, Hegel starts with a single, self-aware individual who faces a world of inanimate objects, and whose attitude develops to appreciate the presence of other people in that world. The modes of knowledge in this section, entitled "self-consciousness," are social, but they remain infected with a strong anti-social quality insofar as relationships with other people involve aggression, domination, and fear.

Three tactics for relating to objects, others, and perspectives, appear repeatedly in this section at successive levels of awareness. First, there is an attempt to *destroy* the alien object, person, or alienating perspective. When that fails, there is an attempt to *control* it and own it. After attempts at control and ownership fail, there is a backing-off, retreat, or *withdrawal* from the situation to secure freedom.

The first, most primitive level of knowledge in this section, is characterized by a feeling of alienation from the world, where external objects stand as a confrontation to one's freedom. To remove these threats, the initial attempt is to destroy the objects. This, however, is soon realized as fruitless: aside from becoming dependent upon the very project of destroying things at every turn, it remains impossible to eliminate every threatening object. The effort to secure freedom consequently shifts to that of owning, or taking control of, the threatening objects, which fails as well: again, aside from becoming dependent upon the things one owns, it remains impossible to own every threatening object.

The next move is to withdraw, which means interpreting the threatening object as something that negates itself. Although the details are vague, Hegel intended that one alters the interpretation of the threatening object to apprehend it as a living, and eventually, self-conscious being. He said this with the background knowledge of how, in an act of self-consciousness, one "negates oneself" in a sense, upon stepping back from oneself and looking at oneself, as when looking into a mirror and seeing oneself, but at a distance. The change in perception here is important and profound, for the external objects are regarded no longer as inanimate, but as other humans like oneself. This renders the prevailing state of awareness social.

The single self-consciousness that is the subject of knowledge is now no longer confronting an inanimate object as a threat, but another human being. This is a more psychologically intense confrontation. Replaying the basic tactics, beginning with that of "destruction," the initial result is a life-and-death struggle where each person tries to kill the other. Hegel is best understood as describing a kind of attitude here, murderous in nature, that resides at the most primitive, animalistic level of human interaction.

At a certain point, with a measure of reflection, the more powerful and victorious combatant in this life-and-death struggle realizes that it is more advantageous to let the defeated fighter live. Rather than kill the equally-murderous opponent, the victorious combatant employs the tactic of "ownership," taking his defeated antagonist as a slave and putting him to work. Aside from the practical advantage of having a worker under one's control, the victorious combatant preserves the defeated one because he achieves a more expanded sense of self through the recognition he receives. The motive is selfish, not moral, and is not a matter of pity. We will say more about the benefits of receiving recognition from another person in the next chapter. The main thought is that if one sets out to kill another person, there is an awaiting realization that the project is self-defeating: once the other person is dead, that person can no longer provide the recognition one had been implicitly seeking.

Despite its advance over the murderous mentality, problems arise in the master–slave relationship, as both the master and the slave eventually find themselves frustrated. First, it is impossible *thoroughly* to control another person or a material object. Second, there is a one-sidedness in the relationship of recognition: the slave respects the master as a "full" person, but since the respect comes from a slave, the recognition has little value to the master; the master recognizes the slave, but recognizes the slave without any respect, as virtually an object to use. The master is recognized in the right kind of way by the wrong kind of person; the slave is recognized in the wrong kind of way by the right kind of person. On both sides, the recognition is incomplete, unbalanced, and unsatisfactory.

As a reaction to the frustration inherent in being either a master or a slave, both parties next employ the tactic of "withdrawal" to secure freedom. Each consequently adopts a detached, distant, and disengaged attitude towards the world and becomes a "stoic." In this transition from the master–slave relationship to stoicism, Hegel appreciated that as a historical matter, somewhat remarkably, the philosophy of Roman stoicism was presented by an emperor, Marcus Aurelius (121-180), as well a slave, Epictetus (55-135). Both masters and slaves were stoics.

Upon withdrawing from the world as a stoic, not much is left to think about in principle, if by "withdrawing from the world" means "not thinking about the world at all." Hegel maintained that this leaves a person empty and in need of something specific to have in mind. Although he was inspired by the Roman Stoics, Hegel also criticized them, describing how they instructed people to be "reasonable," but tended to present their idea of rationality in the form of generalized platitudes.

On a contemporary note, we can add parenthetically that the song, "I am a Rock" (1965), written by Paul Simon, expresses the solitude and loneliness inherent in the stoic attitude well. It describes someone who has chosen to disengage from social life and to retreat into social isolation as the result of a failed love relationship. The person becomes a rock and an island in attitude, expecting to avoid pain as a result.

Philosophically, the stoic faces the dilemma of not being able to think about anything specific, if he remains completely detached from the world, and of sacrificing his freedom if he does engage with the world. To resolve this difficulty, the stoic realizes that he can have something specific to think about and yet preserve his freedom by engaging *negatively* with the world, namely, by saying "no" to whatever is presented as true. This is the disagreeable, nay-saying standpoint of skepticism, which appears to pay off at first sight: when saying "no," one's freedom is asserted and one also has something specific to think about. The tactic employed is once again a "destroying" one, as it follows upon the stoic's tactic of "withdrawal," but instead of people who are destroyed or killed, propositions or perspectives are negated in a more civilized mindset that is nonetheless murderous in nature.

The skeptical attitude cannot endure for long, though, because it leads to confusion. As one says "no" to whatever proposition or perspective presents itself, one's consciousness eventually becomes contradictory. Today I say "no" to some assertion—call it A—and tomorrow I say no to its opposite, *not*-A. Over time, by advocating A and *not*-A, I become mixed-up. The skeptical attitude is a fundamentally unstable one. It is not merely destructive; it is self-destructive.

The skeptic's instability is evident in the two opposing roles it embodies. By saying "no" to any proposition that is presented, he is in the position of the absolute master. By having no control whatsoever over what proposition will be presented, he is in the position of the absolute slave. The upshot is a split and confused consciousness that feels like a master on the one hand, and a slave on the other. Within the skeptical consciousness, the master-slave relationship is now appearing as aspects of a single consciousness, and as the contradiction between these two components comes explicitly into awareness, the skeptical consciousness becomes "unhappy" (*unglückliche*, "unfortunate," "miserable," "sorrowful").

Given its bifurcated condition, the skeptical consciousness transforms into one that appears frequently in religious contexts. This kind of consciousness appreciates that its "master" aspect is, at least in principle, in touch with what is absolute—God, or the truth—while its "slave" aspect constrains it to be a mere physical organism, tiny, contingent, fleshly, and longing for transcendence. In this tension between its soul and its body, it is unhappy. The project of the unhappy consciousness is, from its finite condition, to develop a satisfactory relationship to what is absolute, or God. It seeks a reconciliation between its two opposing aspects.

The unhappy, religious consciousness advances in three stages, each of which brings its finite, earthly, aspect into a closer union with God. In the first of these, the relationship between the human being and God is distant: God is worshipped as a being that exists on a dimension beyond space and time, inscrutable, infinite, and accessible only through deep feeling or devotion. In this mode of religious consciousness, one prays, has faith, does what one believes God wants, and hopes that one is correct without ever knowing the truth.

At the second stage, the relationship between the human being and God is closer: no longer located exclusively in "the beyond," God is recognized as embodied in particular persons and things on earth. This style of religious consciousness can assume a variety of forms. Divine-humans have included emperors, pharaohs, and individuals such as Jesus. Similarly, artifacts associated with divinely-regarded beings are believed to be infused with divine energy. Examples are the worship of saints' bones, teeth, clothes, footprints, and such. Hegel explained the spiritual motivation for the Crusades in these terms, saying that the primary goal was to own Jesus's sepulcher in Jerusalem. To this day, people are fighting over the ownership of holy sites.

Hegel is describing here a general style of thought, where on a more mundane level, one might, for example, believe magically that musical ability could be gained by touching the keys on Mozart's piano, or that wisdom or personal holiness could be attained by visiting the place where some prophet was born, lived, or died. The attitude extends into cherishing the possessions of a deceased family member, as if these items were infused with the family member's spirit. One might visit Hegel's grave in Berlin with the hope of getting inspired to understand Hegel's philosophy, or touch Hegel's desk to the same magical end.

Hegel's Grave in Berlin

Hegel's Desk

In due time, these ways of trying to connect with God are seen as ineffectual: one cannot become a great musician merely by touching the keys on Mozart's piano, or be a person of deep spirituality by sitting under the tree where Buddha was enlightened, or become a leading psychoanalyst by visiting Freud's apartment in Vienna. Neither can one become closer to God by self-sacrificially working the soil as a monk, producing grapes, and making wine, as if the soil, the fruit, the wine, and the earth, were sacred parts of God's body or being. One gives everything to God, but, as Hegel observed, God gives in return only an infinitesimal part, such as a harvest of grapes.

On this quest to become one with God—a quest to realize the divine within oneself, essentially—the oscillation between feeling connected with God, destined for eternity, and feeling like a mere physical being, destined for annihilation, soon reaches its breaking point. One meditates, prays, and feels inspired and connected with the divine, only later to become again immersed into petty routine and worldly preoccupations. While submerged in an experience of cosmic consciousness during a meditation session, one is suddenly interrupted by a need to go to the bathroom.

After oscillating between these two poles of the spirit and the flesh–we can speak of years of involvement here–a sense of hopelessness and a disillusionment with the entire situation emerges. Appreciating that one has been on what appears to be an endless roller-coaster, the sense of disillusionment triggers a sharp disengagement from *both* the spirit and the flesh, the divine and the human, the master and the slave, that leads to a feeling of profound emptiness. Note how the tactic of "withdrawal" becomes operative at this point, following from a frustration in a master-slave structure. This is the "dark night of the soul" where one cares to be neither divine nor human, master nor slave, having experienced how both sides lead to frustration. One arrives in limbo or a netherworld, suspended somewhere between the two, essentially empty and nowhere at all.

Most unexpectedly, this suspended condition becomes the road to salvation and ultimate connection with the absolute, or God, for one's new location is at an intermediary point *between* God and human. Although this is at first a mere point, or a "nothing," the structure of the situation has changed: instead of a back-and-forth oscillation between human and God, a tripartite structure has emerged where God and human are connected through an intermediary location at which the unhappy consciousness is now situated. Regarded positively, this intermediary point is the position that a priest or prophet would assume, as the intermediary between God and the human being.

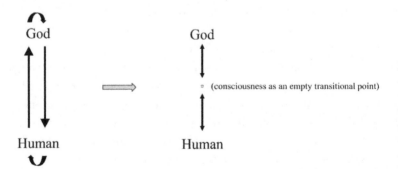

In this way, then, the unhappy, religious consciousness attains a state of awareness where the godlike, or divine aspect of itself can be integrated and reconciled with the human aspect of itself. For Hegel, this introduces a new outlook on the world where one feels at home and in contact with the truth, as one regards this truth as both within and outside of oneself in the external world, permeating the whole situation. He called this state of mind "reason."

Recalling the three main tactics of "destruction," "control/ownership," and "withdrawal" that run through Hegel's discussion, we can summarize the development of knowledge in the section on self-consciousness as follows:

First Phase: (attending to inanimate objects)

Destruction: Destroying all objects

Control/Ownership   Controlling/Owning all objects

Withdrawal: Interpreting inanimate objects as living and self-conscious beings

Second Phase: (attending to other people)

Destruction: Life-and-Death Struggle

Control/Ownership: Master-Slave Relationship

Withdrawal: Stoicism

Third Phase: (attending to one's own self-awareness)

Destruction: Skepticism

Control/Ownership: Unhappy Consciousness as Worshippers/Possessors of Relics

Withdrawal: Unhappy Consciousness as Nothingness; "dark night of the soul"

Reason, Spirit, Religion, and Absolute Knowing

To appreciate the world as a fundamentally rational being—a being like oneself—is to adopt a perspective that makes one feel as if constantly and comfortably looking into a mirror and seeing one's own reflection. On a small scale, it compares to looking at one's son or daughter, and seeing oneself reflected in their bodily structure and behavioral dispositions. It is also like reading a letter that one wrote, seeing one's thoughts inscribed on the page. It is like seeing an old friend at a distance in a crowd, and walking over enthusiastically to shake hands. In these instances, an aspect of the external world acts like a mirror, where one apprehends oneself in objects that are beyond one's immediate presence, leading to a feeling of being at home in the world. There is a unity of "subject" and "object," in effect. When extrapolated to a global attitude, this kind of "mirroring" experience makes one feel comfortable as a participant in the universe as a whole. This attitude is one of "reason," where–although the things in one's experience might at first appear to be foreign–there is an underlying attitude of certainty that nothing is truly alien.

At the level of raw nature–the rocks, stars, air, lightning, rain, mountains, etc.–the rational attitude appreciates nature as having inner purposes or goals, for we ourselves act rationally according to intended plans. This is a "teleological" ("telos" means "goal" in Greek) outlook that one projects onto the entire world, where the world is conceived of as an organically unified being that is growing into maturity according to an inner plan or principle. At the level of rocks and such, the inherent goal-orientedness and associated systematicity of nature remains dim, but it is perceived as implicit, and is appreciated as steadily becoming more manifest as we move from inanimate nature, to plant and animal life, to humanity.

In the section of the *Phenomenology* entitled "Consciousness," the attitude towards raw nature was different. It was mechanical: the physical world appeared there as a set of inanimate items in causal relationships with one another. Their interactions were described completely by a set of natural laws that prescribed their activity as if nature were a series of dominoes clicking away in a rigid and predictable sequence. This mechanical understanding of nature was complete, but it remained inhuman, for the objects involved were conceived of as being thoroughly inanimate. In the attitude of reason at which we have arrived, nature is appreciated non-mechanically as virtually alive and growing. As we can recognize from our discussion of the contents of Hegel's Preface to the *Phenomenology*, this attitude towards the world is distinctively "Hegelian," and is encapsulated well by the phrase, "the rational is the real and the real is the rational."

The third and final section of the *Phenomenology* accordingly outlines a series of perspectives that issue from a teleological, as opposed to mechanical, outlook upon the world. These perspectives refer to raw nature, to begin with, and proceed to the organic world of plants, animals, and individual human psychology. From there, Hegel moves on to discuss various forms of human interaction that are more positively social, in contrast to the more unfriendly forms of social interaction he presented in the section on self-consciousness. These more advanced forms of sociality implicitly, and soon explicitly, reflect an awareness of the "I" that is "we" and the "we" that is "I," namely, "spirit" or properly social consciousness. In this context, he discussed morality, culture, religion, and finally, "absolute knowledge."

To appreciate the change in outlook in this final section of the *Phenomenology*, we can mention one of the first levels of human-human interaction therein that contrasts informatively with the master-slave section on self-consciousness. This is an attitude where a person seeks his or her own selfish pleasure, using other people to obtain it. A smooth-talking seducer would be an example. The attitude is not combative or threatening to the person who is used and it has a manifestly friendly exterior, but the reality is that the user is self-centered and manipulative of others, as if those other people were merely inanimate objects.

A step in advance beyond this pleasure-seeking attitude is the relatively less selfish one where a person is driven by a deep conviction for a cause, believing blindly that everyone else ought to agree and follow along with his or her personal beliefs. The virtue in this outlook, at least, is that it incorporates the rational awareness that everyone ought to be following a general principle, despite how the principle happens to be arbitrary, set merely by the person's own dictates.

From here, the rational awareness that general principles ought to govern everyone equally becomes more intensified. There is an appreciation of the validity of universal moral principles, and this yields a more pronounced moral awareness—one Hegel found effectively expressed by Kant's moral theory emphasizing the importance of acting consistently, i.e., logically and rationally. Still, he appreciated that the simple Kantian imperative to act consistently remains too abstract. To be more realistic, he reaffirmed the importance of living within an actual social community to develop moral awareness. We thus pass from "reason" to "spirit."

Hegel described the various stages of social community according to his standard procedure of starting with more circumscribed forms and moving to more comprehensive ones. He began by discussing the smaller social unit of the family, and moved on to large units, such as the state. He worked through the latter in a progression from dictatorial forms to more balanced democratic ones, invoking Jean-Jacques Rousseau's idea of the general will in connection with the latter.

Despite this gradual advance in social awareness ranging from the selfishness of the pleasure-seeking person to the organized democratic state, Hegel realized that none of these forms, either intrinsically or explicitly, are oriented towards foundational realities of a metaphysical kind. None are inherently geared towards the deepest human questions that concern our presence in the universe and the meaning of existence. Religious communities embody this kind of awareness in Hegel's view, and in this respect, are more advanced in social awareness than moral and political communities. We thus pass from "spirit" to "religion."

Hegel understood religions themselves as progressing historically from those that are more sensuously-based, such as ancient religions that worshipped light, to more recent ones such as Christianity, which emphasize inner feeling and have a greater spiritual depth. Hegel considered Christianity as the most advanced religion, but owing to its reliance upon pictorial imagery, its meaning remains to be clarified into a purer, philosophical form. Upon achieving this clarification, we pass from "religion" to "absolute knowledge," and looking back upon our entire growth from sense-certainty to absolute knowledge, understand who we are as the complete embodiment and realization of "Knowledge" itself, considered as a main personage and leading character of the *Phenomenology.*

6. Hegel's System: Logic, Nature, Spirit

After completing the *Phenomenology* to arrive at absolute knowledge, Hegel set out to develop his more comprehensive philosophical system—reformulating, refining, and extending the ideas he had in mind. Central to his method was the structure of self-consciousness, which he used as the basic principle for his philosophizing. Chapter 2 spoke about the importance of self-consciousness to Hegel's philosophy and we have seen this structure operating in the forms of knowledge in the *Phenomenology*. We can now consider the explicit structure of self-consciousness that had been guiding Hegel's thought throughout—a structure that informs the core of his philosophical system, whose justification and ground he believed was established by the *Phenomenology*'s ascent to absolute knowledge. Only if one philosophizes from the standpoint of absolute knowledge can one's philosophical result have an absolute validity.

When we reflect or think about ourselves, there is an elementary structure inherent in the process: a subject (call it S) thinks about an object (call it O) and recognizes that that object is itself. S realizes that S=O, or that it is thinking about *itself*. We can express this act of self-recognition in a diagram as (S → O → S/O), or pictorially as:

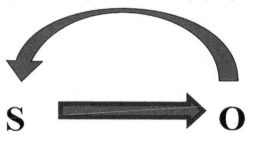

$$\textbf{S} \longrightarrow \textbf{O}$$

In an act of self-consciousness, we start with the initial condition of the unreflective subject, S. Then, there is a projection from that subject, an image or "object," O—somewhat in the way a spider projects a strand of web from itself. This is an image of the subject that the subject then thinks about. As an "object," this image is opposed to the "subject." In an act of self-recognition, the subject then realizes that the object is an image of itself, thereby removing the foreignness of the object. There is an initial "position," a subsequent "opposition," and a consequent "reconciliation" in a three-aspected, sequential, integrated process. This process can be described in several ways, all of which have the same import. It can be referred to as one of "position, opposition, reconciliation," or "position, negation, amalgamation," or, as we find in the philosophical theories of the time, "thesis, antithesis, synthesis." Fichte and Schelling tended to use "thesis, antithesis, synthesis" in their characterizations of the process of self-consciousness; Hegel, less so.

The remarkable feature of this basic structure of self-consciousness is that it can apply not only to the situation when a single person—you or I, or Descartes, for that matter—engages in an act of reflection, as when in his *cogito*, Descartes stated to himself with self-awareness, "I think, I exist." The structure can apply within broader social situations, as when one person recognizes another. Here, the structure of self-consciousness appears at a more expanded level, where the S is the person who is being recognized, the O is the person who is doing the recognizing, and the amalgamation of S and O is the awareness of S as being recognized by O. There is a benefit to S in this process, as we mentioned in the previous chapter. It is what the victorious person appreciates at the end of the life-and-death struggle, and it accounts for why the victor assumes the role of a master instead of killer, deciding to keep the defeated person alive as a slave: in being recognized, one's own sense of self-consciousness is expanded. We can see this in the following diagram through the larger, more sweeping arrows:

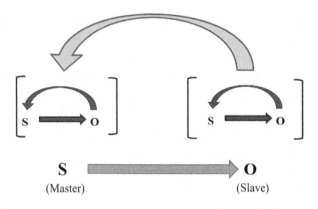

S
(Master)

O
(Slave)

The basic structure of self-consciousness, (S → O → S/O), also appears clearly at the end of the section on "consciousness," where, through scientific inquiry, the fluctuating perceptual field is completely reconstructed and replicated in a set of thoroughly explanatory laws. In this completed set of laws, the perceptual objects that once stood as alien and opposing presences, appear in a reconstructed and replicated form that removes their foreignness. When perceiving the external world, one consequently sees the products of one's own understanding at this level of full scientific awareness.

Similarly, at the very beginning of the *Phenomenology*, in the section on immediate knowledge, the structure of self-consciousness is present when we try to point out the punctually present moment: the "now" as we point to it, dissolves into the "not-now"–namely, a new immediately present moment, and the two moments become amalgamated within the thought of a wider time span that includes them both. This example is noteworthy because the structure of self-consciousness is inherent in the process of knowledge, but we are attending only to passing moments and are not thinking of ourselves.

Hegel showed that the structure of self-consciousness underlies a wide variety of contexts. He maintained that this is the essential structure of reality, and his philosophical system presents the universe as a single act of self-consciousness, where the "S," the "O," and the "S/O" refer to the three ultimate partitions of reality: "logic," "nature," and "human society" or "spirit." Let us now describe this system and its motivation.

When considering the origins of things or of the meaning of life, a common answer to the question, "where did everything come from?" or "why is there something, rather than nothing?" or "what is the point of everything?" is that everything comes from God because God created the world and has a plan for everything—a plan that gives the universe a single, profound meaning. A question that usually follows is "where did God come from," and the standard answer is that God did not come from anywhere, for God always was. Queries then emerge about "why" God made the universe, especially in view of the suffering to which sentient beings are exposed, as from disease or natural disasters.

Some people question the idea that God—conceived of as an all-good, all-knowing, and all-powerful being—could be the source of all things, given the mystery of how a single, intelligent being could exist, to begin with. The being seems to be too complicated, too rich in knowledge, too "mature," one might say, simply to be there all alone from the start, essentially out of nowhere. Also, the reasons God created the world are inscrutable. Since God is said to be totally free, God was not compelled to create the world.

As a social vehicle through which we express our orientation towards ultimate realities, Hegel was sympathetic to every religious standpoint, even though he regarded some as expressing the truth better than others. In contrast to the specifically Biblical account that refers to a supremely powerful, good, and knowledgeable being as the creative source for the world, his understanding of the world's origins aimed to be more explanatory. Adhering to the idea that the universe is essentially rational, and convinced through observation and reflection that the universe is in a process of development, Hegel formulated an account of the universe and its origin in terms of the structure of self-consciousness, which he understood as the most fundamental expression of rationality. Hegel started with the most basic thought—a thought so elementary that we find ourselves thinking of nothing other than totally blank being. This is the bare conception of that which "is," without any content at all. It captures the thought of how God "always was," but in its timelessness, it remains a thought without any specific content. This, for Hegel, is the true beginning of the universe. Nothing can be simpler, because at this rudimentary point, there is nothing determinate about which we are thinking, and in reference to that conception, nothing determinate that is.

The idea of that which simply "is," compares to the conception of empty space or empty time, neither of which has content that fills it. But rather than thinking of empty space or time, Hegel began with thinking of that which is even more indeterminate—nothing but the idea of that which "is," without any content at all. There is nothing more plain and uncomplicated than this idea.

Hegel referred to this initial thought as the pure concept of "being." It was the starting point of his philosophical system, a concept from which he aimed to show the entire universe like a living organism, emerging and growing to maturity. In accordance with the structure of self-consciousness, he described the universe developing in terms of the elementary pattern of "position, opposition, and amalgamation," or alternatively described, "thesis, antithesis, and synthesis." To appreciate this, it is worth looking at how the foundational concept of pure being started everything off.

The first triad of pure concepts

The pure concept of being is completely empty. If we were to say what its content happens to be, we would have to conclude that there is no content, or that the content of the pure concept of being is expressed by none other than the pure concept of "nothing." In this respect, the pure concept of being and the pure concept of nothing have the same content. They are in principle opposed, but at the beginning, they coincide. If we think of one, we think of the other, and they blend together as we think of them. We could even say that the origin of everything is pure emptiness, or pure nothingness, although Hegel did not develop this alternative way of expressing the beginning of things.

Hegel started with the pure concept of being, revealing that in terms of its content, it is identical to the pure concept of nothing, and then reflected upon our thought process when we realize this equivalence. He asked what we would be thinking about upon realizing the simultaneous identity in content of, and yet difference in meaning between, the pure concepts of being and nothing. He wondered what concept would express this amalgamation of "being" and "nothing." With this question, he saw a new concept emerge, namely, the pure concept of "becoming." Whatever is "becoming" is only just about to "be," but it is also more than nothing at all. What is "becoming" is a blend of "being" and "nothing."

This is how the first three concepts of Hegel's philosophical system arise: being, nothing, and becoming. The fascinating aspect of this "first triad" is that these concepts come forth in accord with the elementary structure of self-consciousness: "position" [being], "opposition" [nothing], and "amalgamation" [becoming]. There are no self-conscious beings on the scene here, though. There are only pure concepts whose contents emerge from and flow into one another. From the pure concept of being appears the pure concept of nothing, and from the thought of the two together appears the pure concept of becoming as their blend.

With this first triad of pure concepts, the first of the three main segments of Hegel's system of philosophy–"logic"–begins. As headmaster of the gymnasium in Nuremberg, he wrote the lengthy *Science of Logic* to present this first segment, and then abridged this long book into the first volume of the three-volume presentation of his system, comprised of the *Logic* (sometimes referred as the "smaller" *Logic*), the *Philosophy of Nature*, and the *Philosophy of Spirit*.

Starting with the pure concept of "being," Hegel's *Logic* describes the development of pure concepts—typically those concepts we use in metaphysical speculation, such as "substance," "quantity, "quality," "infinity," "identity and difference," "form and content," "necessity," "possibility," and "actuality"—in an organized, increasingly complicated presentation that he believed to be exhaustive. If there is some concept used standardly in metaphysical speculation, then it, or its close correlate, will have a place in the *Logic* within the development of pure concepts. It will be analogous either to a "bud," or a "blossom," or a "fruit" in the development of pure thought. The *Logic* concludes with the absolute thought, or absolute idea, whose content encompasses the entire process.

In the introduction to the *Science of Logic*, Hegel described the entirety of the *Logic*—somewhat metaphorically, since there is no "God" that is present in his philosophy as of yet—as an exposition of God prior to the appearance of the physical world. This conveys the idea that he is conceiving of the set of pure metaphysical ideas as absolute, and as timelessly foundational to the existence of the physical world.

At the point where pure thought reaches its complete unfolding, Hegel invoked the structure of self-consciousness to explain what happens next: the absolute idea, i.e., pure thought in its entirety, *objectifies* itself, just as a thinking subject objectifies itself when it thinks about itself in an act of reflection. At this cosmic level, the objectification of pure thought appears as "nature," the inanimate physical world. The creation of the world does not happen as the consequence of a decision on the part of a supremely intelligent, good, and powerful being; the physical world appears as the second step—the oppositional step—of the universe's deep-structure process of coming into self-consciousness for itself. The physical world is the immediate objectification of the complete set of pure metaphysical concepts, or the absolute idea, awaiting further development. "Logic" is the initial position, and "nature" is the opposition extending from that original position. A reconciliation, as we can now anticipate, will then follow to complete the process.

The second book of Hegel's philosophical system, the *Philosophy of Nature*, follows the same general pattern as the *Phenomenology* and the *Science of Logic*, insofar as it sets out in developmental sequence, one flowing from the other, the essential concepts that define nature. These are concepts such as "space," "time," "matter," "air," "fire," "water," "earth," "magnetism," "electricity," "chemical processes," "geology," "plants," and "animals." From the simpler to the more complicated, Hegel described the basic features of the physical world.

The third book of Hegel's system, the *Philosophy of Spirit*, presents the amalgamation of pure thought (i.e., rationality; logic) and physical nature, from which human beings emerge. Following what has now become his standard procedure, Hegel initially considered the human being in its more individualistically-centered features, such as raw sensation and psychology, which he called "subjective" spirit. Under the title of "objective spirit," he considered socially-oriented features, such as political and moral outlooks. At the highest level of human culture, he described "absolute" spirit, constituted by art, religion, and philosophy, in that ascending order. We have already seen this developmental presentation of the human being in the *Phenomenology*, except that here, in his philosophical system, Hegel developed the distinctions more clearly. Instead of amalgamating art and religion, and saying little about philosophy *per se* in the section on absolute knowledge as he did in the *Phenomenology*, he separated art, religion, and philosophy into three distinct spheres in his philosophical system and gave an expansive treatment of each.

Hegel's system embodies the structure of self-consciousness in the movement from "logic," to "nature," to "spirit." Reality appears as a single act of self-consciousness constituted by these three components. An attractive feature of this system is that it presents the creation of the physical world not as an arbitrary matter, but as issuing necessarily from the nature of pure thought, conceived of as pure logic. The system also provides a relatively clear answer to the question of the universe's meaning, namely, that the universe is engaged in a process of self-realization. As time goes on, everything becomes more integrated, unified, rational, balanced, free, reconciled, and self-aware.

Logic → **Nature** → **Spirit**

(position → opposition → amalgamation)

(thesis → antithesis → synthesis)

According to this system, the human being stands presently as the most highly developed being in existence, and as we gradually develop socially to intensify our freedom, self-awareness, and mutual respect, we all carry the torch for reality itself. There is no "God" behind the scenes; there is only pure rationality and the accompanying structure of self-consciousness as the underlying substance of everything. If one were to speak of "God," one would speak of the entire universe; if one were to speak of "God's intelligence" or "brain" within the organism that is the universe, one would speak of the human community or "spirit"—namely, the "I" that is "we" and the "we" that is "I," as it comes to realize itself.

The Hegelian style of thinking

Hegel's writings can sometimes be mind-boggling. It is easy for a frustrated reader to throw in the towel and end up with the dismissive joke and with some wit, that Hegel is an absurd thinker whose sentences are longer than his paragraphs. The *Phenomenology* and the *Science of Logic* are especially complex and challenging works that require intense concentration to appreciate their profundity. His early writings and his classroom lectures on world history, art, religion, and philosophy, however, are approachable and enjoyable, while also being informative to read.

Such complications notwithstanding, it is not difficult to understand Hegel's style of thought. Everything he thought about, he regarded as being involved in a process of development from a simpler to a more complicated state. He did not look at a person walking down the street and take that person immediately for granted. Rather, he saw the person as having a history and as having a future. When meeting someone, he did not take first impressions as definitive. He appreciated that to understand a person genuinely, it helps to be acquainted for years in a variety of contexts.

When considering the relative truth of any given philosophy or world view, Hegel tried to see whether its basic principles are vague, abstract, and thin in content, or whether they are determinate, concrete, and rich. An outlook that emphasizes "immediacy" and the "here and now" to the exclusion of everything else—for example, Zen Buddhism—he would understand as an intellectually elementary view that will inevitably break down of its own accord into a more complicated and comprehensive position. A philosophy that emphasizes the presence of arbitrariness everywhere, the absurdity of the world, and the importance of the individual—for example, Jean-Paul Sartre's existentialism—he would understand similarly as undeveloped in its main conceptions. A style of logic that emphasizes exclusionary, "either/or" oppositions—for example, traditional formal logic and mathematics—he regarded as less developed and less appropriate for a foundational metaphysics than a "both/and" style that allows for the integration of opposites and a comprehension of everything.

The following chart presents pairs of concepts that appear frequently in philosophical thought, as well as in religion, politics, art, and social theories. On the left are concepts that Hegel located at the early, immature, elementary, stages of development and awareness; on the right are notions that appear at the more mature and developed stages. The concepts on the left are less highly valued, while the ones on the right do better in capturing the truth.

Hegel's own philosophy accords with this style of evaluation, as it organizes each subject matter that it addresses along this spectrum, starting with the simpler styles of thought and interpretation and progressing towards the more complicated forms. The overall process is from the "abstract" to the "concrete," from the "simple" to the "complicated," from the "less realistic" to the "more realistic," and, accordingly from the "less true" to the "more true." This is the Hegelian style of interpreting the world.

ABSTRACT (-) ═══════════════════════>CONCRETE (+)	
Less True	More True
Less Highly Valued	More Highly Valued

Immediate	>Mediated Simple;
Unarticulated	>Complex; Intricate
Individualistic; Autonomous; Private	>Communal; Social; Public
"Either/Or"	>"Both/And"
Atomistic	>Holistic
Unreflective	>Reflective
Disconnected; Chaotic	>Integrated; Unified
Empty; Superficial	>Rich; Full of Content
Immature; Elementary	>Mature; Developed
One-sided	>Multidimensional
Partial	>Complete; Whole
Generalized	>Specific; Particular
Vague; Unclear	>Determinate; Precise
Limited	>Comprehensive
Finite; Exclusionary	>Infinite; All-inclusive
Unresolved; Tension-Ridden	>Resolved; Harmonious
Unbalanced; Asymmetrical	>Balanced; Symmetrical
Arbitrary Relations of Components	>Systematicity; Organic Unity

7. Absolute Spirit: Art, Religion, Philosophy

Hegel always had a realistic, community-minded outlook on the world and on the nature of philosophy. His early academic life in Tübingen, in Bern, and then in Frankfurt shows this well. In Tübingen, he was impressed by the communal spirit of the ancient Greeks and appealed to it as an inspiration for his conception of a more genuine version of Christianity. In Bern, he briefly relaxed this interest in living communities when he became attracted to Kant's abstract, rationalistic, but also deeply principled moral theory, consistent with Christian morality, since it coincided with the universalistic ideals of the French Revolution. In Frankfurt, he gravitated back into a more down-to-earth romanticist interest in human feeling, and soon, cultivating his historical eye, reworked *The Positivity of the Christian Religion* in 1800, representing in a historical manner the image of Jesus and the idea of what is natural, and appreciating how the communities of different time periods embody different values.

As we have seen, Hegel structured the *Phenomenology of Spirit* with a comparable movement. He began with kinds of knowledge that do not explicitly include human beings, and he proceeded to more human-centered perspectives that develop from individualistic, confrontational, anti-social outlooks into more friendly, cooperative, and communal ones. Religious communities stand as paramount for Hegel in that book, for he discerned within them an intrinsic orientation towards the deepest interests of humanity and absolute knowledge.

When Hegel refined the ideas expressed in the *Phenomenology* and formulated his philosophical system, he separated art, religion, and philosophy into three distinct spheres of human activity, and studied them on their own terms in their respective historical development. Coordinating these three spheres with transitions in the great waves of history, he regarded the cultural spirit of ancient Greece as having a fundamentally artistic orientation. With the appearance of Christianity, he saw this artistic orientation yield to a more religious one. In his own era, he witnessed the religious orientation fade in cultural predominance in favor of a philosophical-scientific style of expressing our most fundamental concerns and understanding of what is true.

These four subjects—history, art, religion, and philosophy—communally considered, were at the forefront of Hegel's intellectual interests during the last decade of his life when he was teaching at the University of Berlin. They were the main topics of his lectures, from which we have thousands of pages of lecture notes. He developed these presentations in conjunction with his interest in political philosophy, writing the *Philosophy of Right* during this time as well, which, concluding as it does with discussions of the family, civil society, and the state, stands as a prelude to the communal expressions of absolute spirit. Hegel's lectures on art, religion, and philosophy present his extended reflections on the three spheres of absolute spirit—the spheres of human community that attend to our primary interests as humans.

Hegel's Philosophy of History

Although Hegel was convinced that reason informs all of reality, he understood that the world is filled with suffering and that this suffering can make the world appear to be meaningless. In traditional theology, the philosophical "problem of evil" is a reaction to this presence of suffering, as it asks with some perplexity why suffering exists if there is an all-good, all-knowing, and all-powerful God. Concerned with the same issue, Hegel answered the problem of evil without reference to a personified God, but in reference to reason itself, explaining specifically why human history is filled with war. He answered that conflict and suffering are a necessary part of the world's growth process towards a more reasonable social condition.

As a matter of philosophical style, Hegel's vision was broad. When he surveyed human history, he looked for large-scale changes that extend from early civilizations to the present, searching for patterns that reveal an underlying rational process, not unlike how a geologist thinks in terms of vast time spans to understand the drifting movement of continents. Hegel thought big, even beyond the typical perspectives of contemporary world leaders and geopolitical theorists who consider the world globally and intelligently as an array of interacting peoples, nations, and corporations, but who always have their own national interests firmly in mind.

Among the patterns Hegel observed was one concerning styles of governments. He noted that as a rule, early civilizations were governed by a single, all-powerful leader such as a pharaoh, emperor, or king. These dictatorships predominated until the times of ancient Greece, when democratic rule emerged solidly, saliently, and successfully to change the spiritual tenor of world history. It is not as if dictatorships suddenly disappeared—they still exist—but rather that the Greeks surpassed the dictatorial style of government, and rendered that style no longer the most advanced in the world.

There were slaves in Greece, though, and not everyone participated in the democratic decision making. The new system of government nonetheless marked an advance by expanding the scope of human freedom: in the early civilizations, genuine freedom inhered in only one person, the absolute ruler. In Greece, freedom inhered in the sector of society composed of free citizens.

For centuries, this was the prevailing and assumed condition: there was a group of free, ruling individuals, and a group of those who were subjugated as workers, subjects, slaves, and subordinates of one kind or another. There was a privileged and powerful class, and there were the common people or subjects. In Hegel's view, the French Revolution of 1789 made a substantial, concrete, groundbreaking change in this arrangement. The theory that everyone is born with certain natural rights had been present in people's minds through the political theories of John Locke (1632-1704) and Jean-Jacques Rousseau (1712-1778), and had been hinted at in Roman Stoicism, but the French Revolution put these ideas into practice and gave them a social reality.

Such ideas were emerging in the spirit of the time. A decade before, the American Revolution came close to achieving a level of emancipation comparable to the French Revolution, writing in its 1776 Declaration of Independence that "all men are created equal, that they are endowed by their Creator with certain unalienable Rights, that among these are Life, Liberty and the pursuit of Happiness." It courageously advanced these liberating ideas, although it remained a slave-holding society in eight of the 13 colonies and still needed to grow.

Hegel regarded the institution of this idea that everyone is free in principle—an idea that came into social clarity in the late 1600s and 1700s—as radically transforming the course of human history and as completing a logical picture: early civilizations considered it rational and legitimate to operate according to the principle that only *one* person is (truly) free. Later civilizations considered it rational and legitimate to operate according to the principle that *some* are free, and contemporary civilizations consider it rational and legitimate to operate according to the principle that *all* people are in principle free. Uneven social arrangements presently exist, and will continue to do so for the foreseeable future, but the contemporary spirit of the times has advanced to a point where their legitimacy is always subject to question.

Implicit in this development is a logical progression from "one," to "some," to "all," the structure of which gives credence to the proposition that human history is developing according to a rational plan. In this light, the history of war reveals itself to be the necessary means to arrive at the universal society—one governed by the awareness that everyone is free and equal, and that slavery of all kinds is wrong. Karl Marx's hope to see exploitation someday altogether removed from human society is an expression of this contemporary spirit.

Hegel anticipated that the future will realize the idea of universal freedom more thoroughly, with humanity integrated into a single, rational, socially-balanced world community. Much can be said and speculated along these lines if we reflect upon the present state of the world. The forces of globalization are intensifying, once-divided countries have been reunified, electronic communications are extensive, and corporations extend their influence across national borders. At the same time, other countries have been broken into smaller parts, and national and ethnic differences remain strong in many quarters. If Hegel's vision of a peaceful and integrated world is to be realized, it is best conceived as a distant one, achieved only through more patience and struggle.

Art, Religion, and Philosophy in History

The section on consciousness in the *Phenomenology* displays an important feature of how knowledge develops: in the movement from immediate knowledge, through perception, to scientific understanding, attention shifts from the external, sensory world to non-sensory objects of thought, which in the case of scientific understanding takes the form of laws of nature, mathematically expressed.

When considering artistic, religious, and philosophical communities in their effort to understand what is ultimately true, Hegel saw the same kind of process. Art, in his view, characteristically expresses the deepest interests of humanity in an external sensory form; religion characteristically expresses them through sensuous mental imagery and feeling; philosophy does so in pure concepts. The movement from art, to religion, to philosophy, has the same basic trajectory as that from immediate knowledge, to perception, to scientific understanding: the expression of truth in pure concepts is achieved through a path that begins in the ordinary sensory world. "Sensation" and "perception," become clarified in the realm of "conception."

Hegel defined the distinctive styles of expressing truth in art, religion, and philosophy by associating them respectively with the external world, mental imagery, and pure conception. For example, he regarded works of art featuring three-dimensional material as their primary medium of expression to be paradigmatic works insofar as their status as "art" is concerned. There are nonetheless many varieties of art, religion, and philosophy, and Hegel accommodated these in his conception of historical development.

Some kinds of art are exemplified by artifacts whose substance and meaning are embodied in solid, three-dimensional objects. For Hegel, they consequently realize art's characteristic style of expression and are consistent with what art ought to be. Other kinds of art, less true to the nature of art itself, are exemplified by artifacts whose substance and meaning are embodied in two- or one-dimensional media. Similarly, some kinds of religion express themselves fundamentally through myths and mental imagery, and exemplify what religion ought to be. Other religions have a stronger orientation towards the external three-dimensional physical world, while still others are more conceptually oriented. It is the same with philosophy: some kinds of philosophy are more focused on features of the external world, others are more imagistic, while still others are more characteristically centered on pure concepts, as philosophy ought to be in Hegel's view.

These varieties of art, religion, and philosophy appear historically, and Hegel described in his lectures how they each arise, grow to maturity, and then decline. There is a historical period when art realizes its characteristic sculptural form, but as history moves on to a period where mental imagery becomes more effective in expressing the deepest interests of humanity, art loses its fundamental cultural role as it gives way to religious expression. Pictorial art, which is more akin to mental imagery, accordingly assumes a more important cultural role at this time to support religious expression.

In the same way, as history moves on to a period where pure concepts become more effective in expressing the deepest interests of humanity, religion loses its fundamental cultural role and gives way to more purely conceptual, philosophical expression. Art first gives way to religion, and then religion gives way to philosophy as the main vehicle for humanity to express its most important spiritual concerns.

As an example, we can consider Hegel's understanding of art, which in his lectures he treated as a sphere of its own, in contrast to how he thought of it in the *Phenomenology*, as fused with religion. In accord with his conception of art as absolute spirit—where, by "absolute spirit," we are speaking of a community that is inherently oriented towards ultimate matters such as human meaning and truth—he defined art as a beautiful mode of expression. He understood "beauty" as the sensory presentation of absolute truth or, more religiously expressed, the sensory presentation of the divine. Art has many functions, but Hegel conceived of it in its most culturally important manifestation, namely, as expressing through beauty, matters of absolute human concern. There are other ways to express the divine, or the absolute truth, but in Hegel's view, art does this characteristically through three-dimensional forms

Architecture and sculpture are the art forms most faithful to what art ought to be, since painting is two-dimensional, music is one-dimensional, and literature is conceptual. From a historical standpoint, Hegel maintained that architecture is the paradigmatic style of art for the pre-Greek civilizations—he referred to the geometrically-formed Egyptian pyramids, whose construction consumed the interests and energies of the entire society—and that the paradigmatic style of art for the Greek civilization is sculpture. One cannot find more idealized and perfected human forms than in classical Greek sculpture, and this is where we find the most beautiful works of art "as art."

Greek philosophy and religion valued the human being above

all other sentient beings, appreciating our rationality and self-consciousness, without at the same time exploring the depths of passion that later characterize Christianity. This created the perfect conditions for art: the abstract forms of the Greek sculptures matched the relatively undeveloped, although strongly human-centered understanding of the human being typical of Greek philosophy and society. Hegel consequently maintains that in Greek sculpture, the material, three-dimensional form coincides perfectly with its spiritual content, and that the finest masterpieces of Greek sculpture—one can see this in their combined strength, serenity, and rationally-idealized forms—are the most beautiful that art, "as art," can display.

Head of Apollo

Hegel's discussion of the Greeks and their beautiful art refers to a time when a certain mentality predominated, but this is not to say that there are no contemporary vestiges of that mentality. There are many cases where old outlooks persist beyond their appropriate time. It is present-day common knowledge that space extends infinitely in all directions and that each star is located at a different distance from earth. Still, when we look at the stars at night, refer to the constellations, and imagine pictures of hunters, horses, queens, birds, scorpions, archers, and such, suggested by the star patterns, we are looking at the sky as if it were a painted dome, as people did centuries ago.

Similarly, we no longer appreciate Greek sculpture as did the Greeks—infused with life, as if the statue of Athena were Athena herself, shining before us with divine energy. Our philosophical awareness has changed, having grown more inward, reflective, conceptually oriented, and distant from the idea of worshipping physical items as a way to come into contact with God, or the absolute truth. Nonetheless, a rudimentary version of this mentality lingers, as when people visit a wax museum and marvel at the apparent presence of some past historical personage brought back to life in simulation, or when they pray to a saint's bones, or to the statue of the saint, as if it were the saint standing there. Some regard the bones and statues as merely symbolic of a higher, more non-tangible reality, but those who worship the bones and statues themselves as objects that are emanating an intrinsic, holy energy, display a mentality that is closer to the earlier, Greek, artistic mode of expressing and apprehending our deepest human concerns.

With the advent of Christianity, with its shift from the ancient Greek focus upon the external world to an orientation towards feelings and mental imagery as its main mode of expression, Hegel considered the religious outlook to come into its own during the Middle Ages, and as such, to define the predominant cultural attitude towards ultimate realities for that period. By the time we reach Hegel's era, roughly from the late 1700s to the early 1800s, with the philosophies of Kant, Fichte, Schelling, and Hegel, he maintained that philosophy—and we can include scientific inquiry here, insofar as it is based on pure concepts in mathematics, and we indeed live now in a scientific and digital era—started to become central in the cultural fabric as an expression of absolute truth.

Whether Hegel was correct about these historical patterns is unclear. But the influence of Karl Marx's communist philosophy, inspired in part by Hegel himself, that spread across the world during the 20th century and influenced especially the societies of Russia, China, and their satellites, provides some evidence that Hegel had a sensitivity to the workings of world history and the emerging influence of philosophy as a world-historical discipline. Insofar as mathematics is a purely conceptual discipline and resides at the basis of scientific inquiry, contemporary culture is being driven by a discipline that is based on pure concepts, since scientific knowledge tends to carry the most authority and truth in our world. Hegel maintained that philosophy proper is the highest discipline that is constituted by pure concepts. Mathematics is a solid step beyond mythology and stands as philosophy's cultural precursor.

One of the notable aspects of Hegel's account of world history is that he formulated it in a self-conscious manner, always sensitive to being able to explain how it is possible for him to construct a philosophical system that expresses the absolute truth. His *Phenomenology* is an aspect of this explanation, as it works through level after level of knowledge until it reaches a fully comprehensive state of absolute knowledge. His philosophy of history as the basis for his history of philosophy is another, as he traced the course of world history and philosophy to a point where his own presence in the history of philosophy emerged as the culmination of a 2000-year development of human thought. Consistent with his own style of philosophizing, Hegel saw himself as a philosopher who is participating centrally in the large-scale movement of philosophical thought in general—"Philosophy" as a kind of personage—and given his understanding of the history of philosophy, justifies his assertion that his philosophy captures the absolute truth.

Some critical reflections

We have been describing Hegel's philosophy sympathetically, aiming to consider his thought as he intended its broad outlines to be grasped. Many questions nonetheless arise, if we turn a more critical eye towards his outlook.

A frequent criticism is the difficulty of disconfirming Hegel's account of history. Suppose one were to argue that the two devastating World Wars of the 20th century, the continued conflicts of the current century, the dramatic increase in electronic surveillance, the prevailing antagonism among religious and political groups, and the persistent threat of nuclear war, all show that human society is not making any real progress in relation to freedom, self-consciousness, mutual respect, and a sense of friendly community.

The Hegelian response—and this is where one can become concerned with the validity of Hegel's view—is that if another worldwide conflict were to occur, then this would not constitute strong evidence that Hegel was mistaken. For such a conflict should be understood as an instance of the second, "oppositional" or "antithetical," phase in the dialectical progress of social growth. Here the critic would point out that this response implies that no historical episode, no matter how awful or devastating, can effectively count against Hegel's view. In Hegel's favor, though, organizations such as the United Nations and more recently, the European Union, have emerged since World War II that aim to foster an atmosphere of cooperation and interdependency between nations. And these are only two of the hundreds of similar examples.

Another criticism of Hegel's thought is more local. In principle, following the structure of self-consciousness, he would ideally describe development in all spheres of life and inquiry as involving a process of opposition and reconciliation, from A, to not-A, to an amalgam of A and not-A. This is not the pattern, however, of many of his own analyses.

Although the three main components of his system, "logic," "nature," and "spirit" follow this primary dialectical pattern of opposition and reconciliation, some of the smaller-scale movements instead have a "rise" and "fall" quality. In his histories of art and religion, for instance, he used a model that refers to an early stage, a mature or pinnacle stage, and a degenerate stage. Furthermore, he sometimes used a "gradual and continuous rise" model, as in the movement of knowledge from sensory perception to pure conception, as well as in the history of philosophy, which culminates in his own philosophical system. Hegel was fundamentally interested in growth, but he called upon three different models to express it, only one of which is dialectically structured.

There is also a Eurocentric quality to Hegel's philosophy. He did not have an extensive knowledge of philosophical thought as it developed, for example, in India and China—a development comparable to Western philosophy in its sophistication. He tended to assume that the early thought in non-Western cultures remained relatively constant in substance over the centuries. This, however, compares unfavorably to referring to Plato and Aristotle as the figures of Western philosophy, requiring us to look no further to grasp the essence of the history of Western philosophy. Such a conception of Western philosophy would render Hegel's own ideas insignificant as a mere footnote to the ancient Greeks.

Another objection, less convincing, is that Hegel's philosophy is essentially totalitarian. When Hegel described the hierarchy of communal organizations in the Phenomenology, the Philosophy of Right, and the Philosophy of Spirit, he began with the family and concluded with "the state" as the most developed political organization. From this, given how "the state" is frequently regarded as an oppressive entity, one might believe that Hegel advocated totalitarianism and that his philosophy supports oppressive and morally objectionable regimes.

We have seen repeatedly, though, how Hegel's conception of the highest form of community—his idea of spirit—envisions people living together with a developed moral consciousness, treating each other as equals, and participating jointly in governmental decision making, as one would have through voting and representatives. Hegel located social relationships that operate according to master-slave relationships—and this can be extended to the relationship between a dictator and a subjected population—at a much lower level of spiritual development, so it is inaccurate to maintain that Hegel's idea of the endpoint of the development of the state would be a totalitarian government.

Another criticism along related lines is that Hegel's philosophy submerges each person into a group collectivity and thereby offends our sense of individual freedom. This kind of view is advanced by those who maintain that everyone is absolutely free and that extensive involvement in communal life is a mere option, not a requirement.

The socially mature value that Hegel placed on community participation issues from his philosophy's foundation in the structure of self-consciousness. He argued that we naturally seek the recognition of other people to expand our sense of self-awareness, and that this naturally leads us into community participation. He would regard any outlook that upholds individuality above community as spiritually undeveloped and contrary to our nature as self-conscious beings.

That we naturally gravitate into communal life does not imply that our freedom must be sacrificed. Ideally, we would all participate directly or indirectly in the formulation of our community's or state's rules and laws, and by doing so, live in accord with laws that we ourselves have helped institute, many of which would include the respect for privacy, freedom of speech, and such. In this sense, we would be acting freely, not as mere individuals, but as members of a genuine community that works together to respect our personal integrity.

The problem is that as the condition of the world presently stands, this kind of community on the wider scale remains a distant ideal. To advance the situation, Hegel would prescribe that people organize to question and reform existing governmental structures for the sake of promoting a more extensive and informed participation of the population at large and a greater respect for individuals. For Hegel, universality and individuality ideally go together, where neither dominates the other.

8. Hegel's Influence

A mong the billions of people in the world, many have never heard of Hegel. Many of those who recognize his name are unaware of his main ideas. Hegel was nonetheless one of the most influential thinkers in the history of Western philosophy and has had a tremendous impact on the world. He is a towering figure within an exclusive league of outstanding thinkers that includes Plato, Aristotle, and Kant. His philosophical stature compares to that of Milton and Shakespeare in the field of English literature, to Galileo and Newton in physics, and to Bach and Beethoven in music.

"Communism" and "Marxism" are household words, but "Hegelianism" is not. Without Hegel, though, there would have been no Marx, for Hegel's philosophical method—one that attends to developmental processes structured according to a pattern involving the reconciliation of opposites—is at the basis of Marx's understanding of human history. The difference is that Marx's orientation is more economically-grounded, for he was convinced that the best way to understand human society is to examine how people work and make a living for themselves.

Marx's view is complex, but Hegel's influence shows itself in Marx's understanding of how, within an elementary capitalist framework, the oppositional relationship between employers, understood to be owners of property, and their workers, plays itself out. In this economic arrangement—we speak here schematically—employers hire workers to make a saleable product, pay the workers as minimally as possible for their labor, collect the workers' products as property, and then sell those products for as high a price as possible. From these sales, employers accumulate profits and grow increasingly wealthier than the workers. As the process continues, the gap in wealth between the property owners and the workers widens, and the workers ultimately become impoverished and enslaved.

As the population of workers increases and the numbers of employers/owners decreases through competition among the employers themselves, the asymmetry between owners and workers in both numbers and wealth reaches a tipping point where the workers rebel, cast out the employers/owners, and assume ownership of the means of production. The workers consequently become worker-owners, and as such, reconcile the former social opposition between the two classes of owners and workers. Marx's debt to Hegel resides in his adoption of a style of analysis that proceeds according to a pattern of opposition and reconciliation.

Marx's ideal end-state–a world commune where there is no longer domination and exploitation of one social class over another–is also indebted to Hegel, for it matches Hegel's idea of the realization of absolute spirit. Hegel speaks of absolute spirit–the full social realization of a global social consciousness characterized by an "I" that is "we," and a "we" that is "I"–with religious overtones, as if it were a society of perfect moral agents, or a society of Jesus-figures. But if we adopt a less idealized and less religiously-resonant version of this social ideal, it will approach how Marx envisioned the perfected human condition. Understanding the word "communism" as "commune-ism" reveals the friendly and cooperative nature of both Hegel's and Marx's visions for the optimal human society.

Marx's theory of history is aptly described as "historical materialism." It contains some dialectical aspects, such as the one described above, but it also includes many non-dialectical features. During the early 20th century, Marxist theorists in the Soviet Union developed a version of Marxism that has more pronounced and thoroughgoing dialectical quality–one closer to Hegel's style of thinking, except translated and transformed directly into a materialist mode, i.e., a "dialectical materialism." If one is familiar with Hegel, the Soviet Marxist literature will strike a familiar chord.

During the same time–the 1930s–Hegel's thought entered French intellectual life significantly through the work of Alexandre Kojève (1902-1968), whose captivating lectures on Hegel–later published in 1947 as *Introduction to the Reading of Hegel*–were attended by the psychoanalyst Jacques Lacan (1901-1981) and the philosopher and phenomenologist, Maurice Merleau-Ponty (1908-1961), among others who became influential in French literature, anthropology, and philosophy. Kojève was an imaginative and profound interpreter, who, understanding Hegel through a Marxist lens, emphasized the superiority of the slave (or worker) in Hegel's master-slave interaction, along with the meaningfulness of world history.

One of the reasons for Hegel's appeal is the amenability of his master-slave discussion for illuminating specific kinds of oppressor-oppressed relationships, such as the man-woman relationship, as explored by Simone de Beauvoir (1908-1986) in *The Second Sex* (1949), and the colonial relationship, delved into by Frantz Fanon (1925-1961) in *Black Skins, White Masks* (1952). Hegel had an insight into the inherent social inadequacy and frustration that enter into all dominance-submission relationships—and these extend from one nation dominating another, one religious group dominating another, and one set of corporations dominating other smaller businesses, to one individual dominating another. No matter where or when one lives, Hegel appreciated that it would not work effectively in terms of our human need to enhance our self-awareness, either at the individual or group level, to be involved in dominance-submission relationships. Only when people respect each other as equals can our humanity shine through properly in a condition of mutual recognition.

What is slowly emerging from this consideration of Hegel's influence is that he is among the most powerful advocates of social integration and equality on a global scale. He understood the necessity of war, but saw it as needed for a future time when universal friendliness would be the rule. This is contrary to the present world and cultural situation where we have sharp antagonisms between internally-integrated social units that are perhaps friendly among themselves and show great spirit in Hegel's sense of the word, but remain hostile to others. We speak here of social oppositions arising from intense nationalism, intense religious identity, intense political party membership, intense corporate identity, and so on, where solid, highly-organized groups of people set themselves against each other.

With respect to this idea of social integration, it is worth mentioning a relatively less known French theorist whose outlook had a strong Hegelian flavor–Pierre Teilhard de Chardin (1881-1955), a paleontologist, geologist, and Jesuit priest, sometimes referred to as the "patron saint of the internet," whose writings were censored by the Roman Catholic Church during his lifetime. From his examination of inanimate nature, plant, animal, and human development that he summarized in *The Phenomenon of Man* (1955), Teilhard apprehended everything developing along a path of increasing integration–one that culminates in a single, human social consciousness. Teilhard's vision is essentially Hegelian, but it has a more contemporary scientific basis combined with a more religious style of expression.

Along similar socially unifying lines, but more temperate and less speculative, Hegel's influence extended into German philosophy of the 20th century, perhaps most saliently into hermeneutics, also known as the theory of interpretation. One of the leading theorists in this field, Hans-Georg Gadamer (1900-2002), understood that the act of interpreting anything involves a blend between what the text (or any item of interpretation) itself says and what the interpreter brings implicitly to the interpretation. This "fusion of horizons" is Hegelian in its inherent optimism: there can always be a "fusion" between opposing views, for no matter how deep the conflict might be with another text, person, time period, and so on, there is always some common linguistic ground upon which some agreement and mutual understanding can be forged. Gadamer's essentially friendly attitude towards interpretation and conversation exhibits an advanced social consciousness in Hegelian terms, quite unlike the skeptic's confrontational, disagreeable, difference-emphasizing "no."

As mentioned, Hegel was himself sensitive to issues of interpretation, for he asked how it was possible for him to interpret human history clearly enough to apprehend the absolute truth that underlies it. In this query, he was motivated by central principles of Kant's theory of knowledge, for Kant emphasized that in our experience we always bring along with us a set of presuppositions from logic, and are compelled to interpret the world in a logical way. Hegel appreciated the inherent logical nature of the world as well, but as we know, he did not regard the appearance of rationality as merely a feature of how humans need to think about things.

Hegel applied Kant's insight in a different way, more historically, understanding that in every interpretation, we carry along with us the spirit of the times in which we live. Today, for example, we are inevitably guided by a set of prejudgments conditioned by scientific knowledge and computerization. Hegel resolved this issue by arguing that he was living in a historical period where the truth had finally revealed itself, while also recognizing a long road ahead during which it would deepen and develop further. Although Hegel's position about living at an absolute point in history is debatable, it stands as a matter of Hegel's influence—and also Kant's—that we can see well in Gadamer's theory of interpretation how our background presuppositions must always be considered when interpreting anything, for whether we realize it or not, our interpretation will contain those presuppositions as an implicit bias.

The critics and neo-Hegelians

We have spoken about Hegel's influence in a positive manner, but there is an alternative way to understand his philosophy's historical impact, namely, in terms of those who reacted strongly against him to develop influential styles of their own. Among his earliest antagonists were Søren Kierkegaard (1813-1855) and Arthur Schopenhauer (1788-1860), both of whom reacted against Hegel's reason-based philosophical system of the world.

Aside from regarding Hegel's system as unrealistic and impossible to complete, Kierkegaard found that Hegel wrote his philosophical system from a standpoint so lofty, that individual people disappeared into mere specks within the great flow of human history. Like a cartographer, Hegel was mapping the terrain of reality itself, and had no time to talk about the structure of the veins on, so to speak, an arbitrary leaf. In Kierkegaard's view, such an arbitrary leaf, however, is what each of us is, and a philosophy that overlooks what we are as individual centers of experience is flawed. On his own tombstone inscription, he wished to have simply the words, "The individual."

As for Schopenhauer, he rejected Hegel's view because he could discern no progress in human history—people fight now just as they did before, only with more powerful weapons—and he could not imagine how creating the perfect society could ever justify the suffering that has already taken place. In Fyodor Dostoevsky's novel, *The Brothers Karamazov* (1879), the character Ivan Karamazov expresses this same Schopenhauerian objection regarding the implausibility of justifying human suffering through an appeal to a future perfect society. Ivan's view is that the terrible suffering of a single infant is not worth it, because everyone else's good fortune does not erase the fact that the infant suffered.

Schopenhauer also disagreed with Hegel's view that the foundation of the world is rational, understanding it rather as a blind and senseless urge, whose materialization as the world of sentient beings doomed to suffer and die senselessly, is a cosmic mistake. Both Schopenhauer and Kierkegaard foreshadowed 20th-century views that regard the world as absurd, as in the French existentialism of Jean-Paul Sartre and Albert Camus.

Hegel's positive influence at the end of the 19th century and the first decades of the 20th extended to British philosophy in a group of figures called the "British Idealists." These included John McTaggart (1866-1925), F. H. Bradley (1846-1924), T. H. Green (1836-1882), Bernard Bosanquet (1848-1923) and R. G. Collingwood (1889-1943). Among their better-known works is Bradley's, *Appearance and Reality* (1893). Although inspired by Hegel, their works have a more contemporary quality and conceptual refinement, and are best referred to as neo-Hegelian.

In critical reaction to these neo-Hegelians were some of their equally-talented students such as Bertrand Russell (1872-1970) and G. E. Moore (1873-1958). Their orientation was more commonsensical, and they rejected views such as Bradley's that asserted the "unreality" of space and time. Soon joined by the philosopher Ludwig Wittgenstein (1889-1951), their work initiated a new style of philosophy—analytic philosophy—that was motivated by new discoveries in mathematical logic by Gottlob Frege (1848-1925), an interest in the philosophy of language, and a respect for the results of scientific inquiry. This style of philosophy became central to 20th- and presently, 21st- century philosophy in Britain and the United States. Analytic philosophy has been a profound, extensive, productive, and rebellious reaction to the Hegelian legacy that continues to this day.

Conclusion

Hegel's *Philosophy of Right* mentions that only in retrospect is it possible to understand the path of world history, since it needed to develop to its present point for anyone to be able to see clearly what had been happening throughout the ages. Hegel said this with an air of sadness, reflecting upon the difficulty of teaching the world what it ought to be. In the past, this was not possible, since wisdom, the "owl of Minerva," flies only at dusk, i.e., after the day is done.

Silver Tetradrachm, Athens (480–420 B.C.E)

Hegel's indeed aimed to teach the world what it ought to be, and if he was fundamentally correct, we now have an idea of what to expect and what to work towards. In this respect, Hegel's remark about the owl of Minerva can be appreciated in a different light: instead of viewing history as having reached a point of closure by finally bringing our universal equality into view, we can understand it as having begun a new day, where everyone knows in their hearts that people ought to be living in a friendly manner together, globally. We are aware that we ought to be going towards establishing a universal, globalist spirit that respects social differences as well as integrates those differences into a genuine community. The endpoint and lesson of Hegel's philosophy, in sum, is the goal of world peace towards which he believed we should all be working. The following image conveys this spirit of Hegel's philosophy well:

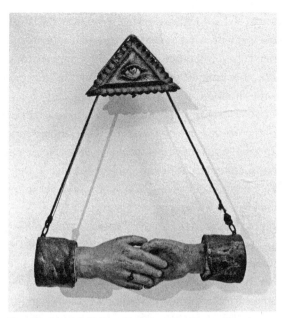

Handshake with the Eye of God – From Steyr, Austria, c.
1800

From our brief survey of Hegel's philosophy, a set of insights and principles has emerged, which we sum up here:

1. It brings us closer to the truth to appreciate everything as part of a larger process that goes beyond the present moment. If we see a child playing in the playground, for example, it helps to envision that child as it will grow into an adult. If one sees an older person sitting on a park bench watching the child play, it helps to remember that decades ago, that person was once a child who played in a playground. To understand ourselves we must understand our history. In contrast, it takes us away from the truth to rest contentedly and confidently with first impressions, with what appears "immediately," with what is

appears as self-evident, with what appears as the latest fashion, and with what appears to be unquestionable. We are always involved in a process, the inherent nature of which is to become more complicated and interesting the more we think about the situation.

2. It brings us closer to the truth to realize that each one of us is part of the world as a whole, that the same natural processes flow through us as they flow through all the trees, clouds, and sky that surround us. When we look at any object, we consequently see ourselves in the object and feel at home in the universe.

3. It brings us closer to the truth of what we are as self-conscious human beings, to relate to others on a balanced and even basis that fosters mutual, equal, and friendly recognition of one another. Dominance and submission relationships are essentially frustrating and never provide the recognition and respect that we implicitly seek as self-conscious beings.

4. It brings us closer to the truth to avoid mistaking the symbols and tokens of our social, intellectual, and spiritual goals for the goals themselves. Merely owning a copy of Hegel's *Phenomenology of Spirit* and placing it on one's bookshelf as a display of intelligence could be self-deceptive; it is essential to study the book and absorb its ideas. Merely placing a statue of the Buddha, or Jesus, on one's table as a symbol of spirituality could also be self-deceptive; it is essential to study the meaning of their message.

5. It brings us closer to the truth to realize that each of us is always growing, and that for every obstacle, there is a path to overcoming the frustrations it imposes. Even when facing death and the termination of one's consciousness, there are alternative ways to interpret the situation, some of which are more positive, stronger, and healthier than others. Growth and development in one's outlook is always possible.

6. It brings us closer to the truth to think concretely, especially about other people. One reads in the newspaper that a person

is an "abuser," "thief," "terrorist," "hero," "patriot," or "humanitarian." Whatever the single-dimensional labels may be, it remains that the individuals are living, flesh-and-blood people—husbands, wives, sisters, brothers, sons, daughters, nephews, nieces, grandmothers, grandfathers—who have done both good and bad in their lives, people who have helped and not helped others upon occasion, people who have loved and hated, people who have had moments of happiness and suffering. Thinking more multi-dimensionally and in a less cartoon-like way, is truer-to-life and more intellectually mature.

7. It brings us closer to the truth to understand that whatever perspective we happen to have, it has its limits, and that it will inevitably grow into a more comprehensive perspective, as long as we experience it to its limit and allow it to break down in a natural manner. No religious, political, or nationalistic identity, for example, is absolute or final in the developing world in which we are immersed. Each perspective will transform into a more mature form as time goes on.

It is a pity that many people scoff at Hegel's philosophy in ignorance and prejudice, for it contains some valuable lessons. They are useful not only for becoming a better person—both as an individual and as a citizen, and for living in greater touch with the truth—but also for helping to realize our shared human interest in living together in peace.

Suggested Reading

Many books have been published on Hegel's philosophy—too many to list here. I have chosen a few helpful and noteworthy books that present Hegel along the traditional lines set forth in the present work.

Lauer, Quentin. *A Reading of Hegel's Phenomenology of Spirit*. New York: Fordham University Press, 1982.

> This book describes the contents of Hegel's Phenomenology in a section-by-section manner. It is clearly written, readable, and does well in being true to Hegel's work. The analyses are accurate and the accompanying historical information is useful, but not excessive. It strikes a good balance between an informal work on Hegel and a highly technical one.

Pinkard, Terry. *Hegel: A Biography*. Cambridge: Cambridge University Press, 2000.

> This is an outstanding biography of Hegel, written in the highly respected Cambridge University Press series of long and detailed biographies of major philosophical figures. If one is interested in finding out some particular details about Hegel's life, this is a reliable book to consult.

Redding, Paul. "G. W. F. Hegel." *Stanford Encyclopedia of Philosophy*. Online at: https://plato.stanford.edu/entries/hegel/

> This encyclopedia article is useful in its exposition of how Hegel has been understood by an array of contemporary Hegel interpreters, some of whom urge that we disregard most of the Hegelian metaphysics, and some of whom resist this anti-metaphysical movement. It also contains a good bibliography for further scholarly reading. The *Stanford Encyclopedia of Philosophy* is noteworthy in its mission to present articles that represent the cutting-edge of

scholarship, so they are useful for discovering what has been happening recently in academic research.

Solomon, Robert C. *In the Spirit of Hegel*. Oxford: Oxford University Press, 1983.

This is a comprehensive presentation (668 pp.) of Hegel's *Phenomenology* by an excellent writer and philosopher, done in a conversational, approachable, yet academically-informed style. It is a pleasure to read.

Stace, W. T. *The Philosophy of Hegel: A Systematic Exposition*. London: Macmillan Publishing, 1924/Dover Publishing, 1955.

Straightforward, sympathetic, and complete expositions of Hegel's system of philosophy are rare. These days, they are out of fashion. This book, originally published in 1924, gives a reliable presentation of Hegel's Logic, Philosophy of Nature, and Philosophy of Spirit in a single volume. It comes with a useful, large-sheet, "Diagram of the Hegelian Philosophy"–a real gem–that provides an overview of the system in its entirety.

About the Author

Robert L. Wicks is Professor of Philosophy at the University of Auckland, New Zealand. Prior to his appointment at the University of Auckland, he studied Hegel's aesthetics as a Fulbright Scholar at the Hegel Archives in Bochum, Germany, and taught philosophy at the University of Wisconsin-Madison and the University of Arizona. He is the author of eight books and numerous essays on late eighteenth- and early nineteenth-century philosophy, most of which focus on the philosophy of art and metaphysics.

A Word from the Publisher

Thank you for reading *Simply Hegel*!

If you enjoyed reading it, we would be grateful if you could help others discover and enjoy it too.

Please review it with your favorite book provider such as Amazon, BN, Kobo, iBooks and Goodreads, among others.

Again, thank you for your support and we look forward to offering you more great reads.